When the Fairy Tale Fails

How Women Today Can Create Their Own "Happy Ever After"

When the Fairy Tale Fails

How Women Today Can Create Their Own "Happy Ever After"

By

Susan E. Indenbaum, MSW, LCSW

New Horizon Press
Far Hills, New Jersey

New Horizon Press
P.O. Box 669
Far Hills, NJ 07931

Susan E. Indenbaum, MSW, LCSW
When the Fairy Tale Fails:
How Women Today Can Create Their Own "Happy Ever After"

Cover Design: Robert Aulicino
Interior Design: Susan Sanderson

Library of Congress Control Number: 2006923963

ISBN 13: 978-0-88282-281-5
ISBN 10: 0-88282-281-0
New Horizon Press

Manufactured in the U.S.A.

2009 2008 2007 / 5 4 3 2

Dedication

To my husband, who over the years has supported me through much change and personal growth. To my sons, who I pray will always live with faith and purpose, valuing women as equals. To my precious Aunt Pipi, who always modeled congruency, never once distracted from her life's purpose. To my wonderful girlfriends and my sister Dottye—all have been a constant source of encouragement and support. Thanks.

Author's Note

This book is based on research, a thorough study of the available literature and experience counseling patients, as well as my clients' own real life experiences. Fictitious identities and names have been given to all characters in this book in order to protect individual privacy and some characters are composites.

Table of Contents

Introduction xi

Chapter 1 What's a Nice Girl Like Me Doing in a Place Like This? ... 1

Chapter 2 The Loss of Self…One Little Piece at a Time 23

Chapter 3 Have a Midlife Crisis—Lord Knows You Need One! 43

Chapter 4 Retrieving the Lost Self—Reclaiming the Real You 65

Chapter 5 What Women Long For 81
(And it Hasn't Got Anything to do With Sex)

Chapter 6 The Grouping Trend of the New Millennium 105

Chapter 7 Finding Your Passion—What Passion? 119

Chapter 8 Finding Your Faith—Rekindling Your Spirit 141

Chapter 9 Sex, Lies, and the Midlife Marriage 153

Chapter 10 The Affair: A Major Fairy Tale Buster..................................177

Conclusions..201

Introduction

It really was a fairy tale…I suppose that many of you have figured that out by now. I can't believe that we bought into it, can you? But we did, and young women still do buy into it today. They are, however, destined to have a wake-up call one day when they have to face the hard, cold truth: Prince Charming just isn't going to make them happy after all! Many women will experience this "awakening" as a midlife crisis, but some will be lucky to reach this turning point before they hit that marker. I hope to awaken a few more.

Now, if I ask any intelligent woman if she believes in fairy tales, she'll give me a raised eyebrow and an unequivocal "no." Yet we all grew up listening to familiar fables like Cinderella, Snow White, and Sleeping Beauty, while dreamily waiting for the "happily ever after" that graced each ending. My favorite was Cinderella. I was completely mesmerized by the flowing gowns, the magic, and, of course, the flawless, handsome prince. I suppose these "rescue" stories appealed to our girlish desire to be swept off of our feet with the promise of eternal bliss, and it certainly appealed to our childish belief that it could all happen magically. We didn't just listen with our ears, though; we listened with our hearts and minds, unwittingly internalizing a belief that we could find happiness if we just found the right man.

Although this magical gift of eternal happiness would appeal to almost anyone, it was not offered to just anyone in the fairy tales; it was a present offered specifically to a woman, a woman needing rescue by a man.The rescuer was strong, holding position and power, whereas the "rescuee" was weaker, lacking power, and therefore had a dependent, "less than" status. There is a subtle implication that the woman in these stories *needs* to be rescued in order to be happy. Some young girls, even in our enlightened age, grow up internalizing this story of being rescued by a man, and it is this partly unconscious belief or expectation that now drives much of their adult behavior as it relates to their relationships with men.

A backdrop of patriarchy fueled the fairy tales and belief in a male rescue for women. Efforts to prevent women from positions of power, to control finances, to treat women as if their opinions weren't valid, or to treat women as "removers of the dirt" only served to feed a woman's belief that she was dependent on men and could not experience her own separate meaning, happiness, and purpose in life. This book begins by addressing these patriarchal attitudes and the fairy tales that impact our beliefs and feelings about ourselves as women.

As a psychotherapist, I know that what we believe about something will determine much of how we will feel about it. If I believe that a situation is dangerous, I will feel fear. If I believe that I have lost something valuable, I will feel sadness.

Likewise, if I believe that I am "less than," I will feel unworthy, doubtful, and unsure of my own thoughts, feelings, or words. If I doubt my own inner voice, believing you are superior, then I will likely "give up and give in" when you disagree with me. I will give up my own beliefs, actions, or words to please you if I feel several notches down on the totem pole.

Here's where the real trouble lies. Women who start out in relationships believing they are "less than" are repeatedly "giving up and giving in;" they start to give away who they really are one little piece at a time. And if you have given up who you really are, then you become less and less familiar with the person you started out to be. How can you find your purpose, be true to your own values, or find something you're really passionate about if you're not really being you anymore?

In my counseling practice I see many women who are resentful and depressed as they struggle in their middle years to cope with great disappointment and disillusionment.They often reach the age of forty only to find that the happiness they expected did not last forever, because they have put all of their hopes, dreams, and energies into a man, they now feel empty, lost, and unfulfilled. The internalized belief in "the rescue" led these women to sit back on their laurels and wait passively for men to make them happy. They didn't prepare themselves mentally and spiritually to build on their own passions and dreams in life, the fulfillment of which brings true contentment. "But I haven't been sitting back on my laurels," you might say. "I have done everything to keep him happy." Maybe that is the problem.

Through my clients, I not only see women's despair, I also see them start to awaken as they recognize the loss of their true selves, then change directions and begin taking responsibility for finding their own happiness and meaning in life. Some women don't have a clue where to begin; they have been afraid of standing up for themselves for fear of being abandoned. They must first learn how to demand respect and set clear boundaries with a partner. As soon as women quit blaming men and accept responsibility for their parts in enabling the perpetuation of these old patterns, they can begin the journeys back to their true selves and move forward in their searches for purpose and meaning in their lives. You don't have to leave your partners (which is what most women fear) in order to be your authentic selves.

I have come to feel passionately about women—their "less than" status, their give-away of selves, their need for female friendship, their lack of personalized faith, and their lack of purpose in their lives. Many books strive for political correctness and therefore deny or trivialize the real female experience in a patriarchal society and the effect that a "less than" status has had on women and their personal pursuit of happiness. Too many women today are still looking to men for fulfillment, purpose, and happiness. And too many women today are living someone else's dream, acting on someone else's beliefs, and saying "okay" when they mean "no way."

This book is for all women young and old who have experienced a "less than" status in their relationships with men, those who have given up and given in too many times. I am writing for all of those women who struggle with loneliness and desire friendships with other women. Women are empowered and validated by other women. This book is also for those of you who feel a lack of purpose or faith, and therefore experience a void in your spirit. It is not a book that simply tells you what you are lacking or what you need, but it will give you the "how to's" for rediscovering your true self, friendships, faith, dreams and purpose, and hopefully, how to have a little fun in the process.

I have written what I believe is a realistic view of the midlife marriage which is troubled, not the pie in the sky, idealistic version that we see and hear about in the media. It is fear of abandonment or divorce that holds many women back, but I want to show you how you can change and grow without leaving your partner. I want you to see that the possible outcome is well worth any risk that you take. Changing yourself is the best way to spur change in your partner.

Are you ready to take back the responsibility for your one and only life? If so, you are ready for this book. You'll never know who you can be as long as you're living someone else's life. If you are tired of resentment and disappointment and ready to work on you, not him, you are ready for this journey. I have helped hundreds of women wake up, take the reigns, and become who they were meant to be. Now I want to help you!

1 What's a Nice Girl Like Me Doing in a Place Like This?

It Really Was Just a Fairy Tale, Wasn't it?

Jackie looks tired and frazzled as she rushes into her therapy session about fifteen minutes late. She plops down in the chair next to me and quickly spouts off dozens of excuses for her lateness. I glance down at her patient information sheet to discover that she's only thirty-eight-years-old, yet she looks weary, like someone who's ready to cry "uncle" in the middle of the ninth round. At second glance, I read that she is employed as a sales representative for a large drug company, and I notice that her address is in one of our most upscale neighborhoods. After she catches her breath and adjusts her eyes to the soft light in my office, she starts to tell her story, the reason she is sitting in a therapist's office.

By the end of the hour I've learned that Jackie works forty hours-plus a week but still feels responsible for ninety percent of the housework and childcare once she gets home. She has no time for friends, because her husband pouts if she asks him to watch the kids. He sits on the couch and watches sports while she does dishes and laundry, and she hasn't been to church in nearly a year because he likes her to stay home with him on Sunday mornings. (She shifts uneasily in her chair as she relates this fact.) After twelve years of marriage she finds herself feeling tired, disappointed, and resentful. "It really was a fairy tale, but it's gone awry," she says.

It was clear that we could talk for weeks about her husband's shortcomings, and it was equally clear that she didn't like it when I tried to shift the focus back to her own behavior in response to her husband's selfish or inconsiderate ways. I was hoping that she would be able to "get it" and that she wouldn't be scared away as I shifted the spotlight in her direction. Jackie was unwittingly enabling the very behaviors that prevented her needs from being met, and nothing was going to change until she accepted that responsibility and changed her part in it.

So many of the women I see in therapy look tired. Some of them are still quite young; they have the latest hairstyles, high-paying jobs, and nice houses in upscale neighborhoods, but they all seem thoroughly exhausted. Like Jackie, they have awakened to a scene that is quite different from the dream they had as starry-eyed young girls. Prince Charming doesn't seem so charming anymore, and the "happily ever after" doesn't feel so happy after all. They look weary from going to work and taking care of the house, the kids, and the husband who can't quite figure out how glasses fit into the dishwasher or how socks make it into the laundry. Just how does a charming, intelligent, fun-loving girl with a heart full of dreams end up feeling so tired, disappointed, resentful, and trapped? What happened? And why is she feeling so guilty for even having an occasional fantasy of running away to the Fiji islands?

Women as "Less Than"

As a psychotherapist, I have begun to see an all too familiar pattern among women when they come to see me complaining of depression, or a general sense of restlessness and dissatisfaction with their lives. I usually find, however, that the focus of therapy revolves around the men in their lives (or their desire to have men in their lives), not on *themselves* or what they can do to improve themselves. Many women have worked so hard for that "perfect catch" only to be depressed and disappointed about the realities they now live in day after day. As therapy progresses, it becomes clear that these beautiful, intelligent women started out feeling "less than" in relationships with the men that many had so diligently pursued. They rarely saw themselves as equals in intelligence, status, or success. They lacked confidence that their own opinions were as valuable as their partners, and tended to give in and give up their own beliefs, desires, and needs, and slowly adapt their spouse's.

As we moved forward in therapy, it became evident that these women continued to behave in ways that perpetuated a "less than" position in their relationships. I repeatedly had to ask myself why these bright women ever felt "less than" in the first place. But I didn't have to look far; I looked at my own life and had to admit that I too had been caught up in the fairy tale. My heart, not my head, held fast to the belief that a man was my rescuer, my source of happiness. I started out in my relationship with my husband of thirty years feeling "less than" and acting "less than." As a result, I started to give up things I valued, believed, or needed in order to please him.

Fortunately, as I approached age forty, I woke up; my midlife restlessness prompted me to begin a journey to rediscover my old self, my true self. I now realize that giving up things that I truly believed in didn't work, and would have led me further into a loss of self, followed by resentment and misery, had it gone unchecked. I also realize now that my husband was attracted to the real me, and could have handled my boundaries and assertions of beliefs and needs from the very beginning.

If a woman loses her real self bit by bit in order to be in a relationship with a man, then I believe she will miss out on finding her own passion and purpose in life. She simply won't be *herself*; she'll be living someone else's life. And if she starts a relationship feeling "less than," chances are greater that she will get caught up in "giving up" and "giving-in" behaviors that will change who she is, or who she can become. So *why* do women start out feeling less than men in relationships? Why did I, a college graduate, an extrovert, a leader, begin to doubt my own thoughts and behaviors when I fell in love with a man? Do women have a bigger problem with low self-esteem? Can we simply chalk this up to women's caregiving qualities? Are women just more giving than men? I don't think so.

Before we can address this loss of self and the road back to authenticity, we need to look backward to the origins of a woman's place in our society. There are three factors that need to be explored in order to understand the reasons why women start out in relationships with men believing (even if unconsciously) that they are "less than." We need to examine *society's tales*, the *fairy tales*, and *men's tales*.

TALES TOLD BY SOCIETY

Patriarchy is a Thing of the Past

We are still living in a patriarchal society. A man's time and accomplishments are given more value than a woman's—that's the essence of patriarchy. Elizabeth Dodson Gray, author of *Patriarchy as a Conceptual Trap*, says, "A conceptual trap is to the thought world of the mind what the astronomers' black holes are to the universe. Once inside, there seems to be no way of getting out or seeing out. A conceptual trap is a way of thinking that is like a room which – once inside- you cannot imagine a world outside." But, you ask, didn't we get out of the patriarchal "hole?" Don't we have equality right here in the good old USA?It depends on who you ask.

I experience little bits of patriarchy almost every day. It hit me recently when the bank called our home and asked to speak to my husband. I asked who was calling and they said, "This is BB&T calling to tell Mr. Indenbaum that because he has a mortgage with us he is eligible for…blank, blank, and blank." I said, "Well, I'm Mrs. Indenbaum and my name is also on the mortgage and I happen to pay the mortgage, so what do you have to offer me? The woman was so shocked, she didn't know what to say. I wrote a letter to the bank's executives reminding them that women are earning money and putting money in their bank and that they needed to revise their outlook. I told them that I worked and actually made the mortgage payment, and I expected to be treated as an equal by the bank. They sent me a pen as a consolation gift with a short apology letter. I wouldn't be surprised if they were still calling the "man of the house" with their offer of prizes. Why? Because for many years men were the only ones earning money to put in the bank, and from then on men have been making significantly more money than women. Bank executives therefore came to think of men as their most valued customers. And we must never forget that in modern society money is power.

Here's another everyday example of modern-day patriarchy. I send a contribution to an organization for a cause that's really important to *me* and they write back and thank my husband for the contribution. Now I know that his name is printed at the top of the check along with mine, but it would *behoove* officials to look at who signed the check! (My friend, Carmen, wants to write a book of "Behoovioral Science.") One animal rights organization called yesterday and asked for Mr. Indenbaum. After I told the person that he wasn't home, he started to leave a message regarding who was calling. I asked why he was phoning Mr. Indenbaum and he informed me that it was because of his past contributions. I then informed them that Mr. Indenbaum has never sent them any money and probably never would, and that they were doing a great injustice to women when they fail to acknowledge their contributions.

You might be mumbling something about this being awfully petty, but it's the continuation of all these little things (and there're millions more) that perpetuate the very serious notion of women as less important. It continues to amaze me that so many women want to ignore or deny the fact that these old patriarchal attitudes still exist; they want to see them as most men do: things of the past. It certainly wouldn't improve society if women came to dominate men, and I don't think that's what most women want. Most women just want and need equal respect, which, of course, is most clearly demonstrated through actions, not words.

Men Are in Charge of Our Protection and Survival

There are conflicting theories about whether our society began as a patriarchy or a matriarchy, and the truth is that we'll never know for certain. Archeologists who support the theory of an initial matriarchy believe that women in prehistoric times were once seen as "godlike" due to their abilities to bring new life into the world. They believe that when men discovered that they had a role in this "new life" process they then felt more powerful, and thus began the shift in power. Others theorize that women lost power when men began the custom of removing them from their groups, the other women in the "tribe." As they took them away, one by one, for marriage, the women's groups broke up and women began to lose their power. These matriarchal societies were theoretically not competitive; they worked together for the good of the group while supporting the individual's own pursuits. If society was ever matriarchal (and we can't really be sure that it was), I bet there was a balanced budget and no weapons of mass destruction!

Marilyn French, in her book, *Beyond Power*, talks about women's early solidarity and the connection of mothers with daughters and granddaughters and sisters with each other. It was this *grouping* that gave women power and influence. She supports the theory of an early matriarchy which disappeared over time, with women losing their political and moral power when their groups of related women were broken up. This matriarchal theory espouses the notion that by *isolating* women from each other, men gained power and supremacy over them. I see this as a critical point for women because we have become increasingly isolated over the past century and are just now starting to approach a new era of female connectedness through women's groups. I'll talk more about the women's grouping trend in Chapter 6.

Behavior doesn't always *continue* for the same reasons that it *began*. I can certainly believe that men, due to their superior physical strength, may have started out as protectors of women, the physically weaker sex. I can even see how, as protectors for reasons of survival, they may have come to dominate and feel superior. It stands to reason that if early man needed not only his wits, but also sheer physical strength for survival, that men, would be superior.

However, it is clear that what may have started out as protection turned into domination for reasons other than survival. Not wanting women to have an education, to vote, to own property, to have bank accounts, to hold high-level jobs or have equal pay...well, it simply isn't about protection anymore. The position of power became increasingly comfortable for men, and although there were no more bears, tigers, or lions to fight, they didn't want to give up power over women. When our basic survival needs had long been met, men no longer protected, but fought to prevent women from pursuing higher-level needs—needs for meaning, purpose, and status. The "fairy tale" only helped to perpetuate women's false hope that men were rescuing them and taking charge of their best interests.

Whether you espouse the theory of an initial matriarchy or a patriarchy, the truth remains: When all was said and done, men ended up in a position of superiority over women and, in many societies, have remained there until this day.

Society Hails Women as "Removers of the Dirt"

Most women don't grow up fantasizing that some day they will clean up after others. After the prince comes along, we think we should be a "princess"...with the gown, the crown, and maybe even a servant or two to order around. I'll never forget when I first heard the term, "removers of the dirt." Sometime in the mid-eighties I was invited by my friend, Louise, to attend a women's conference presented by Elizabeth Dodson Gray, author, environmentalist, futurist, and feminist theologian. She talked about how women became removers of the dirt while men sat around the village gates creating the myths and establishing the rules. It was suggested that men in prehistoric times had the freedom to go out of the home and create human "culture" because they weren't involved in bearing and caring for the children.

Yesterday in therapy, Cara, a seventeen-year-old girl told me about her problem saying "no." When I asked her to give me an example, she told me that her brother (age nineteen) and his friends are always asking her to get them a drink or bring them a snack when they are hanging out at her house. She at first told them they can get it themselves, but when they kept asking, she gave in. She confided that her mother "spoils" her brother who doesn't ever clean up after himself or know how to do his own laundry. It was clear that this young woman was learning through her mother's modeling that she should wait on and clean up after men. She will probably behave the same way with her future husband, acting out the continuation of a role—one we need to lose—"remover of the dirt."

Our modern society continues to enable and perpetuate this image of women as "removers of the dirt" through the power of the media. For years, movies and television shows have portrayed women as sex objects or Susie homemakers, lesser positions for sure. Television commercials show ads for cleaning products where women are hailed for their dirt-removing capabilities: "*Mama* knows the power of clean" (and daddy doesn't know___! I can't help but add). My least favorite television commercial is an advertisement where they show a helpless, disgusted-looking father addressing his small children, who have just made a mess in the kitchen. He whines, "Where *is* your mother?"

Women everywhere are saying that they are tired of being the maid, and midlife women say that what they want more than anything is to take care of themselves for a while. But is society really improving if we have to wait until we are fifty and our kids are leaving the house before we can have this kind of respect for ourselves? Are we modeling for our children the very thing that we want to change for women? Are we acting out the "remover of the dirt" role and then expecting our children to do it differently? Men who want women to be the "removers of the dirt" devalue them, and women who accept that role devalue themselves, feeling "less than," acting "less than," and becoming "less than" they could be.

THE FAIRY TALES
Mr. Right Will Rescue You and Make You Happy

We don't have to look all the way back to the stone age to see the male myth system at work in our society. Let's move along a million years or so to the fairy tales by the Brothers Grimm. They did their bit to perpetuate the myth of male superiority and women as "less than." We were raised on fairy tales like Snow White, Cinderella, and Sleeping Beauty, where the female was always rescued by a charming prince who then magically blessed her with a happy ever after. Tale number one: You can be rescued by a man. There is no rescue. Tale number two: You will live happily ever after if you locate Mister Right. In reality, there is no happy ever after; life is difficult, and probably more difficult if you consciously or unconsciously think that someone else is going to rescue you and make you happy.

I wonder how many of us realize the psychological impact that these "stories" had on our expectations, hopes, and dreams for the future. Not hopes in our own qualities or abilities, but hopes in someone else's. I remember lying in bed conjuring up images of my future prince. In elementary school I sat in class and drew pictures of Cinderella's beautiful ball gown instead of listening to the teacher explain how cells divide. Oh, how I longed for that dress!

We were brought up on these and other fairy tales where the prince literally sweeps the princess off her feet, and then magically provides her eternal happiness. Not only is that one of the biggest lies ever told, is is a lie with generations of consequences. I believe this is the root of women's irrational thinking about finding happiness through a man. Society had failed to teach me that I'd be better off lying in my bed planning how to make my own money or how to engineer and build my own dream house, a house that I *might* want to share with a man. The myth of happiness through a male rescue cheated women out of learning the needed skills for creating their own happiness.

It became a self-fulfilling prophecy: Women believed men would provide them with the things necessary for happiness, so they didn't bother to equip themselves. And because we didn't equip ourselves with the skills to provide, we *had* to rely on men to provide for us. *Choosing* to rely is quite different than *having* to rely. Having to rely makes us "less than."

A Familiar Fairy Tale

Like most females, I woke up one day shocked to realize that the fairy tale was actually a myth. I was left feeling resentful and somewhat trapped, similar to the many women that I see in therapy. It goes like this: She meets Prince Charming and fails to see his shortcomings, due to the blinders of romance and the overshadowing dream of "the fairy tale." You know exactly what I'm talking about. The fantasy is so big that she can't quite see that he has a little problem with telling the truth. She rationalizes that he lies because he is afraid of losing her, and anyway, he says he'll never do it again. She turns down a chance to go to college or a chance to train for a better paying position because he doesn't want her to go far away for so long. She rationalizes that he loves her too much to let her go, so she marries him instead.

About year seven the prince gets caught in additional lies, and she finds out that he has a younger princess on the side. She is working hard to make the marriage endure because they have two adorable chil-

through her husband and his accomplishments, not in who she is, and what she has to offer. Her current contribution might be childrearing and housekeeping, but if she doesn't *know* the value of her work and see herself as an equal partner, then neither will her husband. I'm not proposing that women go out there and get power jobs to buy themselves a luxury car, but I am suggesting that women *choose* their "job"—childrearing or bank president—and then recognize its value. A person's worth is not really determined by our salary–that's a tale.

The fairy tale leads women to not only count on acquiring material things through men, but also to look to men for intangibles such as success or status. Sometimes I do a little exercise in therapy with women who are anxious or depressed as they put their lives on hold waiting for Prince Charming. I first have them list all of the qualities they are looking for in a man. Then I ask them to tell me what they would like to be if their wildest dreams could come true, or if magic were possible. The list of characteristics, qualities, or things that they acknowledge as what they would like to become is usually the same or similar to the list of qualities they have sought out in a man. Yet all of their energy has gone into pursuing a man who has these qualities, not in trying to gain these things or qualities for themselves. It is so hard to get women to see that if they spend half the energy they use trying to "catch" successful men on becoming successful themselves, they'd be so happy—with or without men. Instead of simply looking for men who have integrity, confidence, education or a successful career, they might be better off putting their energy into "becoming" full of integrity, confidence, education, and working to be successful themselves.

MEN'S TALES
Your Value is Determined by the Size of Your Paycheck

I know women who have chosen to be homemakers who have great self esteem and respect from their spouses. They recognize the value of the qualities they have and the value of their contribu-

dren. But things just aren't the same. She can't quite afford a clea person, so she goes to work everyday and then cleans the castle or weekends while Prince Charming is off playing golf. The cute, traits that attracted her to the prince are now driving her stark ra mad. His recklessness with money was great when he was taking he exotic places to impress her, but now she wants to strangle him for "i sponsible" spending.

"She Made a Good Catch"... Just Part of the Fairy Tale

Yes, she made a good catch, but she never learned how swim, so if she falls out of the boat, she'll drown. The implication is th the woman is the lucky one. She's lucky to find a good rescuer wi great potential to bring her eternal happiness. Being in this predic ment, however, can leave us feeling disappointed and disillusionec "But," you may say, "I'm in no predicament; I have a $550,000 house, new luxury car, and a husband who lets me do whatever I want." Whe I hear these words in a therapy session, I always wish the woman cou hear herself sounding like a child referring to a benevolent parent. Ye you may be "allowed" to do a lot, but are you really your *own* person

A husband who "lets" his wife spend an evening with h friends doesn't change the fact that someone is master and someone subject to the master. Thirty-five year old women with college degre tell me what their husbands "let" them do. The power differential is blatant. When women believe, and *act* like they believe, that they kno for themselves what they can and can't do, then they will no longer se permission from men. When we act like we have the sense to call o own shots, we will be treated that way. We tell our children that we w treat them like grown-ups when they act like grown-ups. In much t same way, when women act like they're as valuable as men, they will treated as if they are as valuable.

In the prior example, the woman believes her value com

tion. But I see many more women who think that because they haven't been bringing home a paycheck that they don't have the right to ask for much, or that their ideas, beliefs, and opinions aren't as valid as their husband's. They have allowed their worth to be determined by men. Another tale: "Whoever has the biggest paycheck is superior."

So many women in their thirties or forties have come into counseling and told me that they have lost their senses of worth after working as homemakers for a few years. I don't believe this is totally about these women and their personal lack of self esteem. I see it as a societal problem, a symptom of our system, which values a job more in terms of the dollars it produces. Women have gotten many subtle, and not so subtle, messages implying that the work that they do—keeping children safe, clean, fed, and surrounded by an orderly, loving environment—just isn't as important as a man's paid job. Each of us has to take responsibility for changing the way men value the hard job of managing a home. I heard Maria Shriver say on a talk show the other day, "We must stop saying, 'I'm *just* a mother. '"If I *behave* as if my job is as valuable as your $100,000 job, then you will have to treat me that way. It's hard to believe, but many college-educated women who care for their children in the home still get an "allowance" from their husbands. Women who see their contributions as equally important will more likely share equal access to family finances.

If women continue to buy into the men's tale that we aren't as valuable if our work doesn't produce dollars (or as many dollars), then we hold ourselves back, changing who we are or who we can become. If I believe that I'm "less than" and I act "less than," it causes the world to treat me as "less than." Then, when the world treats me as less, I say to myself, "I must be less" and then I continue acting as if I'm less. See what a vicious cycle we're in? We can't wait for society to change, but *we* are society and we must change!

"Don't Worry— I'll Give You Everything You Need"

Since men have historically controlled the financial world, there are many lingering patriarchal attitudes that perpetuate a "less than" status for women. The most obvious way that men tell us that we are "less than" is through the handling of money. In my therapy sessions, a common husband's response to a wife who is complaining that he controls all of the finances and keeps her in the dark is, "I don't know what she's unhappy about, I give her everything she needs." This implies of course that the giver is the one in control. It is through his benevolence, not through shared power and access, that your needs will be met.

In the business world a full partner can have access to all information and participate fully in decision making. When a woman asks for equal participation and knowledge of family finances she is acting like a real partner. Marriage works best when it is a partnership. Nonetheless, women are treated as less than partners when they are given the message that they just can't handle financial matters. If there is a legitimate problem with a woman's history of handling money, then she should take responsibility for fixing her problem so that she can participate responsibly.

Sometimes I hear men tell women that they cannot participate in making decisions about money because the men are protecting them from worry. Well, I don't know about you, but I'm likely to worry more when I don't know what the heck is going on! Keeping someone in the dark is a way of gaining power over them, not sharing power with them. A man who takes full control of finances so that you won't have to "worry your pretty little head about it" simply wants to remain in control. A woman who cooperates by not challenging this position simply enables and empowers him to stay in control. Ignoring or accepting this patriarchal attitude simply perpetuates our "less than" status.

A few years ago our financial advisor (who normally met with both me and my husband) had a private meeting with my husband, and advised him to open up a new investment account. When he brought him the paperwork to be signed, I learned that the account was to be set up in my husband's name only. I called this advisor and told him that I couldn't understand why he did not put the account in our joint names like our other investments. His response was, "I don't know what you are worried about; if you get a divorce, you will get half of it."My response to him was, "I don't plan on getting a divorce and I want half ownership of our resources now. Would you be comfortable with your wife having all of your investments in her name only?"I knew the answer to that question. We now have another financial advisor.

Men Just Know More

Another way that men tell women that we are "less than" is in the weight they give our voice or opinions. The false assumption that a man just knows more is one of the biggest reasons that women "give up and give in" to men. My girlfriend told me the other day about a conversation she had with her husband and a group of male engineers. A retaining wall in her yard was deteriorating and they were discussing the problem of having to cut a road in order to haul the dirt and equipment needed. They were showing her and her husband where they planned to cut a road, and the expense that it would add. She piped in and pointed out that if they would cut the road further down by the tree line, it would be much easier and less expensive. She said they kept on talking as if she hadn't spoken. Again, she interrupted to point out her idea about an easier route. She was again politely ignored. Two hours later her husband told her that the engineers had decided that they would cut the road down by the tree line. There was never any acknowledgement that this was her idea from the very beginning.

"The Dumb Act"

I get discouraged about the rate at which things are changing when I hear my adolescent son and his friends joking about a woman's place in the kitchen. Somehow in our enlightened society they have learned well that men want to be waited on by women, and at age sixteen, they very much want to be "men." It comes out with a laugh or a snicker because they also know that it is politically incorrect. My son has been doing his laundry for some time. The other night we were talking about laundry when he told me about a conversation that he had with one of his male friends. He said that when his friend's mom told him he would have to do his own laundry, the father, with a wink and a grin, told him that if he wanted to get out of doing it, he should put one of the red towels in the wash, and since everything would come out pink, his mother wouldn't let him do laundry anymore. He also told my son that his father advised him when he got his drivers license, "If you don't want to have to run errands for your mom, when she asks you to get some baking powder, you should get baking soda, and next time she'll just run out and get it herself." Believe it or not, many women still fall for the "dumb act" and seriously believe men are incapable of doing laundry or other simple household chores.

I heard the best example of the "dumb act" the other night when my son's friend told him about senior week at Myrtle Beach. He and seven other guys had rented a house together, and he was laughing about how they had trashed it. He said that they called some girls and invited them over, and then when the girls arrived, they asked them to help clean up the messy house. He said the guys "pretended" that they didn't know how to clean and, "We got the girls to clean it for us." It was obvious by his laughter that they got great satisfaction from playing the dumb act.

I get frustrated sometimes in couples therapy when after weeks of counseling the woman has finally learned to ask assertively for her husband's help with the household chores. She then asks that he help with laundry, only to have him pathetically answer that he doesn't know how. I suggest that she instruct him and assume that since he is intelligent enough to run a large business he'll quickly catch on. He comes back the next week sheepishly shrugging his shoulders while his wife tells how he botched the laundry all up. He just couldn't tell darks from lights and just couldn't fold a rectangular towel. He couldn't figure out what was white and what wasn't, so he placed all of the whites and colors together and her underwear came out gray. At this point, most women will give up and do the wash themselves in order to get it done right, falling prey again to *the dumb act*.

I wasn't the least bit surprised when I heard on *Good Morning America* that the "Chore Wars" were affecting couples' sex lives. When you know in your gut that he's purposely doing a chore wrong so that you won't ask him to do it again, you get rightfully resentful. Resentment builds. The thing that women seem to resent most is asking or telling their spouses what to do. Let's face it, he isn't dumb, and you know darn well that he sees the mess as well as you. Today, many enlightened women have clarified with their spouses what they will and will not take on regarding chores; some have actually gotten quite creative in their solutions.

I'm not too sure that I should admit them, but I'll tell you a couple of strategies that I've used in dealing with males in my house when they have failed to pick up their own messes. In our early years of marriage my husband never (he'd prefer I say "rarely") put anything back in its place. I tried nagging and the usual cajoling, but nothing worked. (Nagging never works.)When I nagged, he told me that he would get around to it, indicating that he had full intentions of picking the thing up…sometime. I felt resentful if I picked up after him, but I also resented it if the mess was left there and I had to look at it for days. One day I bought a nice deep basket for his stuff. Anytime I found his things lying out of place around the house, I just swept them into the basket rather than figuring out where they belonged. At the end of each day I placed the basket in his closet where I couldn't see it. When he started hollering, "Where's my______", I just reminded him to look in the basket. It wasn't a perfect solution, but I felt more in charge of my own happiness; I took action, and in doing so was one step away from "less than" in my relationship.

There are many ways to get the "dirt" removed if family members refuse to assume some responsibility. When finances allow, take responsibility for hiring help to get the job done. You might tell the family what sacrifices they will be making (movies, special snacks, activities, etc.) in order for you to pay for house cleaning help. I love the way a woman acquaintance (in her fifties) gets her small house repairs done. She tells her husband about a repair that needs to be done. Then she tells him that if he can't get to it by such and such a date that she will arrange for a repairman to do it. He tells me that this prevents any nagging, and if he doesn't want to spend the money, he has to take responsibility for getting the task done before her deadline. Pretty clever!

DIDN'T THE WOMEN'S MOVEMENT FIX EVERYTHING??

Similar to the Civil Rights movement of the 1960s (which didn't fix everything), the women's movement of the seventies was just the beginning on a long road to a realized equality. The briefest review of women's history ought to take into consideration the activists that worked so hard for us in the sixties and seventies. Although women still experience the residual effects of being treated as "less than" by men, we certainly made some important legal advancements through the women's rights movement. Now I know that some old enough to remember might be thinking, "They were extremists and I didn't want anything to do with that."But if we're honest with ourselves, we'd have to admit that it usually takes the "extremist" to get the attention of the public before any "shake up" of the established system can take place. It takes a lot of courage to step out of mainstream thinking (orchestrated by men) and demand something different in the face of demeaning criticism.

I'm going to be honest and confess to you that I slept through the whole women's revolution. I remember hearing about the attention-getting activities like the bra burnings, but I was young and easily influenced by my conservative elders, and as a result, I ignored the whole thing. Now I realize the value of the fight and appreciate the flack that women like Betty Friedman and Gloria Steinem took from their opponents. I realize too that I didn't have to agree with every detail, every method, or every proponent, in order to do my part in fighting for the principle. My midlife memory fails me, but I, like so many others, probably feared being labeled a "feminist."

In one interview where Gloria Steinem was asked why women are afraid to be called "feminist," she answered by saying, "They either believe in the traditional position of women (beneath men), they just don't understand the word, or they are afraid of the punishment that it will bring."She goes on to say that,"If we say we're for equal job pay, that's reform; but if we say we're feminist, that's recognizing women as inferior (as in a caste system) and that requires a basic, much more extensive kind of change. Change scares us, and, it's usually a lot of work. But I think it's our fear of disapproval from men that scares us the most. It scares us, because we lack belief in ourselves, and this lack of trust in ourselves is reinforced by forces outside of ourselves."

CHOOSE A BIGGER POT

Women get stuck doing many things just because "it's always been done that way," even when it clearly no longer works for us. Do we really have to stay stuck in our habits and patterns of behavior once we recognize they aren't working for us? One story may better explain what I'm trying to say. One day a young bride was cooking her first pot roast as her husband watched. Before she put the roast in the pot she used a carving knife to chop off the outside piece."Why are you cutting off the end of the roast?" asked her husband. She explained to him, "I cut it because my mother always did it that way." So she went to her mother and asked, "Why did you always cut the end of the roast off before you put it in the pot?" Her mother said she did it that way because *her* mother had always done it like that. They went to grandma and asked her why she cut the end of the roast off, and grandma said, "I had to cut the end off because I didn't have a pot big enough to hold a whole roast."

That's how I see the role and expectations of women today. We're expected to do what generations before us did while taking on new roles. We can't see that it just doesn't fit the pot anymore! The reasons why things were done the old way no longer exist. Women are tired and depressed because they are caught between patriarchy and an actualized liberation. They are working outside the home while still taking on eighty to ninety percent of the housework and childcare. They hear and read that they are liberated but don't experience it in their everyday lives.

When I first heard the term "superwoman" applied to the modern female that I presumed myself to be, it sounded so powerful. Attached to that term, however, was the meaning that the superwoman would and could do it all. As the well-respected TV show guru Dr. Phil says, "What were we thinking?" Did we not "get it," that doing it all meant working outside the home and doing all of the childcare and the housework too?

As a result, many women are trying to do it all and are just frazzled— clinging to the roles and behaviors of a patriarchal society while struggling to adopt the new ones. It's not that we mind being *"a"* remover of the dirt, it's just that we don't want to be *"THE"* removers of the dirt. Being "the remover of the dirt" makes me "less than," but being "a remover of the dirt" makes us equals. One implies that we are participating in a job belonging to *all*; the other implies that the job is mine, *my* responsibility. It takes a while to realize that we can choose, not fall, into our roles. Women notoriously choose or fall into their roles to please others, not themselves. Is this working for us? Is this bringing us happiness? Or do we end up feeling "less than?" If we believe and act like a messy house is a reflection on us, and not our spouse or big kids, then we are accepting the role of "remover of the dirt" as ours and ours alone. Do we really want that title all to ourselves?

Women can choose their roles, and we are responsible for our choices. The roles and behaviors that I choose determine whether I end up feeling "less than" or "equal to." A lot of women I know have chosen to work full-time outside the home; it makes them feel satisfied with themselves. Others have quit or gone to part-time work in order to take control of their very busy lives so they won't be as frazzled. Even more women are hiring housecleaning help as a way of alleviating themselves from that responsibility. If I'm home full-time, then I see the housework as my "job" from eight to five, but it's a joint task after five and on weekends. If we are both working outside the home, the housework is our *joint* task twenty-four seven.

QUESTIONS AND SUGGESTIONS

Question: Do you feel that you are treated as an equal in your relationship with your partner?
Suggestion: If the answer is no, stop and write down your partner's specific behaviors that you believe are contributing to a "less than" status (i. e., withholding financial information). For each behavior identified, write an assertive statement that says how this particular behavior makes you feel and what action you need him to take in order for you to feel like an equal in this partnership. Now tell your partner.

Question: Have you been acting as "*the* remover of the dirt" in your home, and working outside the home as well?
Suggestion: (1) Sit down with your spouse and calmly discuss your feelings and needs, being very specific and clear about what you need from him in order to feel of equal value. For example, you might say, "It makes me mad when you lie on the couch and watch TV while I straighten the house and start dinner after work. I need for you to help straighten up the house so we can relax together after dinner. Can I count on you for that?"Be sure to be specific about what chores you

want him to do and then follow through. If you say that you will not pick his clothes off the floor any longer, be sure that you don't give in to the temptation to do it. (2)Sit down with your children and explain everyone's responsibility for "dirt removal." Give them specific tasks for individual "dirt removal" as well as communal cleaning. For example, give your child specific instructions about what is expected regarding his cleaning up after himself, and then add at least one duty that is for the benefit of all (like emptying the kitchen garbage).

Question: Can you identify an organization, such as your bank, community government, or charitable organization that is treating you as "less than?"
Suggestion: Tell yourself you will act assertively next time you feel you are being devalued by any organization. Decide how you will politely tell officials that their behavior devalues you as a woman, and then tell them how their behavior could change in order for you to feel of equal value to their male customers. For example, a letter to your investment firm might say, "When you address marketing letters or financial information to my husband only, it makes me feel that you don't value me as a client or recognize my influence on our financial decisions."

2

The Loss of Self… One Little Piece at a Time

Who the Heck is that Stranger in the Mirror?

Too many women wake up in their thirties or forties to see reflections in their mirrors that they barely recognize, and don't really like. They have become more of a reflection of their spouses than the vibrant, young people they used to be. They have taken on their likes, their dislikes, their senses of humor, their styles, or their values. They have allowed the men in their lives to cause them to question themselves and doubt their own beliefs, even their own feelings. Just why does a highly intelligent and charming woman like you get caught up into changing herself to please a man? When does it begin, and how does it happen? And why does it take so long for a woman to recognize that her old self, the person she really is, has slowly and silently slipped away?

I used to be funny
I used to be so creative
I used to wear such fun clothes

I used to be close to my sister
I used to have really great friends
I used to have a strong faith

I hear these remarks every day as I'm listening to the women that I see in therapy. "I used to have girlfriends, but my husband didn't like most of them, so I just gradually lost touch with them." Or, this is a familiar one," I used to wear really fun clothes, but my boyfriend didn't like for me to dress like that, so I started wearing what he likes." I also hear this statement a lot. "I used to go to the beach with the girls for the weekend once in a while, but my husband gets mad if I ask him to watch the kids for that long, so I haven't done it in years." (As a result, she's looking like someone who hasn't had a good rest in years!) One woman told me that her husband frequently smoked marijuana, and so after a while, although she didn't like smoking, she started using it too. She used to love to go to church, but her husband wanted her to stay home with him on Sundays, so gradually she stopped going. She had to admit that she really had no clue what she liked or didn't like anymore; she had given up her own preferences little by little in order to please her partner. She also had to admit that she didn't particularly like the person she sees in the mirror now.

WHY DO WOMEN CHANGE THEMSELVES FOR MEN?

The stage is already set—a patriarchal society and the fairy tale have set you up to believe that you are "less than" and you'd better make "a good catch." Young women are subtly "programmed" to look for their happiness, meaning, or status through finding the right man. Although it's easy to see how our patriarchal society has already conditioned them to feel somewhat "less than," there are clearly other factors that contribute to the giveaway of the true self. Women might begin to "give up and give in" to men because of other obvious inequities in status. It can be an inequitable educational status, social status, or even physical appearance. Anything that makes a person feel slightly "less than" is increasing the likelihood that she will placate her partner by giving in and giving up even her most basic values or beliefs. Since historically men have had more education, money, and job status, it is more likely that women will feel lower in status.

Unequal Status in Job, Finances, or Education

A lot of doctors marry their nurses; business executives fall for their secretaries. This scenario can cause a status differential that may lead the men to feel like bosses over their wives, and often leads women to feel subjugated to their husbands. Very few women can maintain confidence and emotional independence when there is a large gap in job or educational status (assuming that she's on the "lesser" end). Knowledge is power, and she presumes that he must know more. (And he very well may know more about dentistry or dermatology, but that doesn't mean he knows more about what's right for you.)

I have been treating Gail, a forty-one year old woman, who is feeling miserable and depressed. She is a stay-at-home mom living in a beautiful house with what would appear on the surface to be a "charmed" lifestyle. She had grown up in a home where her father abandoned the family and her mother supported them by working in a grocery store. She never thought about college as a possibility for herself, but because of her beauty, she was able to work as a model for a while in her early twenties. In her travels she met a doctor who swept her off her feet and provided her with a lifestyle that she couldn't have imagined. He had a doctorate in medicine and she had a high school diploma. How can a high school graduate dare to question a doctor? She recalls how early on in their marriage she used to lie about her education when they were in social situations, as "he seemed embarrassed about the truth. Lying made me feel even worse about myself." As time went on she felt "stupid" as she allowed him to control the money, which gave him even more power over her. But, as she settled into the lifestyle, the thought of losing it all became more frightening, and something to be avoided at all cost. Thus, the stage is set for the "giving up" and "giving in" behaviors that lead to the loss of the true self.

Status can come from social standing, family background, or financial standing, as well as through intellectual, educational, or career status. Jennifer, another woman I see in therapy, allows herself to be controlled by her husband's family's social status and her desire to fit in and please not only him, but his family. She succumbed to extreme pressures to behave in ways that were totally against her values, preferences, or wishes…. all to please the socially empowered. She lived in horror that her background would become known in her mother-in-law's social circle. Her husband treated her as "less than" and she just kept trying harder to please. She ended up in therapy because she was not feeling that ol' happy-ever-after, and she didn't like who she was becoming. She was not using her education because he wanted her to stay at home and prepare nice hors d'oeurvres for entertaining the right people. After the excitement of buying all the right furniture wore off, she got bored and struggled to find meaning. He didn't want her to worry her little head about finances, so he controlled all of the money and gave her a small allowance. If she showed any signs of restlessness, he bought her something pretty. Her allowance is now being spent on therapy, in an attempt to figure out who the heck she really is.

Fear of Abandonment

Given the hierarchy that developed way back when, and the fairy tale with its happy hereafter, it's no wonder that women are so afraid of abandonment. The fairy tale said that I had to be rescued, and if I might scare the rescuer off by feeling the way I feel and thinking the way I think…then I guess I'd better change the way I think or feel. So, when I am just being myself, and start to do something that is just "me being me," I don't know what to think when Prince Charming over there makes a face and says, "honey, I don't want you to dress like that" or "you don't need to go see Carol, because I don't like her, and I'd rather you stay home and spend time with me." Well, I sure as heck don't want to make the man who is supposed to bring me eternal joy mad, so I'll just give up this one thing to make him happy. Well, that one little thing turns into forty little things before you know it, and before you even realize it, you're somebody who looks and acts like somebody else. Pretty soon you even forget what you used to be like before you changed to please Prince Charming.

I never cease to be amazed at just how frightened women are of abandonment by men. A woman's "one down" status makes her feel lucky to have him and she fears that he'll run off screaming into the night if she dares to stand up and say "no" to him. Now I know women come by this fear honestly. For centuries women had no means of supporting themselves, and having no husband meant destitute circumstances. I wish I could say that women with no income and no formal education or training are the only ones that fear abandonment so much, but I can't. This old long established fear of being without a man leads capable women to behave in ways that enable their partners to control them and rob them of their true selves.

No one likes the idea of abandonment but, as I tell my anxious clients, "fear" and "not liking" are two different things. I also teach them that we overcome our fears by moving toward the feared object and facing our fear. Giving in to fear leads to avoidance, and in this case it means avoiding anything that might tick off our partner. Choosing to do pleasing things for your partner is one thing; avoiding standing up for yourself because of fear of abandonment is quite another. If you tell lies or swear too much and your partner asks you to change that behavior, you might think to yourself that this change would probably be in your best interest. In other words, this change in behavior wouldn't go against what you know in your gut is good for you. However, if your partner tells you that it's a waste of time when you announce your desire to finally take an art class, giving up and giving in might not be in your best interest.

If a woman feels good enough—smart enough, pretty enough, etc.—she'll be more willing to risk her mate's annoyance when she speaks her own mind or stands up for what she believes. In other words, confidence leads me to stand up for what I really need, believe, or value. The risk of abandonment is usually overestimated in a woman's mind since her "not as good as" beliefs about herself are more fiction than fact. We've all seen it; some of the prettiest, most personable, or smartest women in the world lack belief in themselves. Their beliefs are not rational; likewise, their fear of being abandoned is most often irrational. Take Princess Diana, for example. Maybe she based her worth on how her husband treated her, or how the royal family treated her, not on the factual evidence of who she was, or what the public thought of her. Many women don't know their own strength or worth, but they think they know his. They tend to underestimate their own worth and overestimate his.

I'm Okay as Long as He's Happy

So we start out as bright-eyed young women brought up on the promise and hope of the fairy tale. We're betting on that "happy ever after" ending. We also believe, ever so naively, that we should do whatever it takes to keep our man happy if we want things to work out. Therefore, we start to determine our own adequacy based on how happy *he* is, not on our own knowledge of ourselves, our values, or our own qualities or accomplishments. There are two major errors in this thinking. One, we can't make someone else happy, and two, did we not consider that if we had to give up our own needs and desires to make someone else happy there would most certainly be no "happy ever after" for us?

In a recent research project groups of little girls and little boys were each given a large, beautifully wrapped package to open. The researchers had placed pencils and erasers in the box instead of something exciting or fun. The boys (videotaped separately) opened theirs and voiced a loud show of disapproval over the school supplies. When the girls opened theirs, they acted very pleased and made comments about what a nice gift it was. The girls wouldn't risk disapproval by voicing a negative opinion to the gift givers. They were more concerned with the feelings of the gift-giver than their own feelings. The researchers then gave sour, unsweetened lemonade to the group of boys who openly made contorted faces, some even spitting their drinks out. The girls tried to control their physical reaction to the sour drink and commented on how good it was, while making a polite excuse when offered more. They tried the same experiment on college-age men and women and even the college-age women pretended to like the sour lemonade whereas the men made comments like, "you forgot the sugar." Women are socialized from infancy to please others. Girls are told to be "nice" a hundred times a day. Women are historically predisposed to feel "less than" by society and then socialized to be "nice" about it.

If we're in a society that declares men to be of greater value than women, then we mistakenly believe that we are more valuable if we have men in our lives. We then believe that in order to keep these men, we must keep them happy at all cost. We try to prove our value by thinking and behaving like somebody else wants us to, not how we really are. If I think that I'm okay only *if* you're okay with me, then I have to give up and give in to keep you happy. But, if I realize that my worth doesn't depend so much on your approval or reaction as it does mine, then I'm less likely to change just to keep you happy.

Isolation Just Makes the "Giveaway" Easier

Women who are isolated from family and friends, particularly those friends that have known them since birth, are at increased risk for becoming "someone else." Your family serves to remind you about who the "original" you really is. They know you and will comment if they see you acting or thinking in ways they know just aren't "you." (We're assuming here that your family is not off-the-scale dysfunctional.)If someone is treating you badly, but justifying it with "it's just you, you're paranoid," then your family or long-time friends will hopefully set you straight. Lora, a young mother who I see for counseling, lives several states away from her family and lifelong friends. She didn't want to worry them, so when she talked to them on the phone she always told them that things were fine. Finally, when she was so anxious that she could hardly eat or sleep, she told her mother and father about some of the things that her husband had been doing for years—how he convinced her that she is not smart, is incapable of handling money, and could never hold a job. She went on to tell them that he won't even let her buy a pair of jeans without his permission, he checks her voice mail, he calls her several times if she leaves the house (even to go grocery shopping), and he tells her which friends she can or cannot associate with. Her family was able to validate what she knew in her gut and give her the support she needed. She was then able to get into counseling for more support and validation.

Unfortunately, some women won't listen to their parents' or family's feedback about such things and, let's face it, some families just don't have good judgment. However, some women are lucky enough to have relatively healthy families as well as friends to reflect back their true selves. When a supportive family is lacking, women can certainly reach out to their friends. But if we quit spending time with friends in order to please a man, we lose not only the fun of social contact, but also possible validation for our true selves. If the main feedback about who you are comes from a man who wants to change you, then you're getting faulty feedback and will gradually become fooled or confused about who you really are. A weakened you could become convinced that new behaviors, looks, or attitudes are improvements, and that you will only be happy if you are doing the dance that makes Prince Charming happy. When women allow men to isolate them from friends and family, they might as well kiss their old self goodbye!

Like most young college graduates, I never lived in the same town as my family after meeting "mister right." The man I married was certainly not a bad person, but he was surely my opposite, and he definitely had a lot of ideas and beliefs that were different from mine. He had a strong personality and more education, and like most women, I started out with an internalized belief that I was slightly "less than." When he was offered a job halfway across the country, I gave up my acceptance to a graduate school in Virginia to follow him to Nebraska—far from my South Carolina roots. Then we had our first child hundreds of miles from my home. I had few women friends in this new place, and no sisters or any family for support. When I look back at it now, I see how isolated I was and how influenced by my husband I was; influenced to change in ways that I probably wouldn't have if I had family and women friends around me.

I became much more vulnerable while isolated from those who knew the real me. There was no one there to challenge me, to question any new way of thinking and behaving, or remind me of what I've always known and been. It seemed like the farther I got from home, the more I doubted myself, and the more I trusted my husband for the answers to life's questions. I gradually created distance between me and some of the things that I knew to be true. When I did listen to my gut, I'd allow him to convince me that I was wrong. I let his voice override my inner voices.

WHEN DOES THE LOSS OF SELF BEGIN?

Dating

Research confirms we learn as little girls to gain approval by pleasing others, even at the expense of losing our own values, needs, beliefs or dreams. As soon as girls become interested in boys, they begin to change themselves in order to gain approval. The giving up and giving in behaviors that change who we are usually begin early in the dating phase of a relationship, and few recognize the early signs. The romance and clouded view of how we *think* things will be often has little to do with reality.

One of my pet peeves occurred with a close friend a few years ago, who after being single for a long time, started seriously dating a guy. We would usually talk several times a week on the phone and our relationship was very important to me. But as soon as she got involved with a man, the phone calls all but stopped. The time she spent with other girlfriends dwindled as well; she spent all of her free time with him. I experienced a sudden vacuum where our friendship had been. The fairy tale had swept her away and she put all of her time and energies into her prince. The courting was fast and furious and when it was over and the wedding vows were spoken, the prince began to change. To make a long story short, he turned out to be nuts and the relationship ended. It was the support of her friends and family (whom she had abandoned) that she needed now.

And so it begins…a woman abandons good friends and supportive family in order to pursue the fairy tale. Instead of including the man into her existing network, she exits completely in hopes of finding the happy ever after. You used to have Sunday dinner with your family, but he doesn't like to go, so you give it up. You used to play tennis with your girlfriend on Saturday, but your new boyfriend says he wants to learn, so you stop playing with your friend who has rearranged her whole life to get away from the kids on Saturday mornings. You have always volunteered at church to teach vacation Bible school in the summer, but he says that he can't stand to be away from you for five nights in a row, so you tell them you're not available this year. And so it goes.

The other extreme exists as well. Have you ever had a girlfriend start dating someone and try to include him in everything she does with friends and family? She never visits her sister anymore without him. She shows up at girls' night out with him. She has lost her individualism, and although she tries to hang on to friends and maintain family relationships, it's always as a couple, never as an individual. What is she afraid of? Why doesn't she just say, "No, this is girl time and I'll spend time with you another night?" I had a teenager tell me in therapy the other day that she only sees her girlfriends when they all go somewhere together with their boyfriends. She admitted that she spends almost no time with her girlfriends now that she has a boyfriend. She also admitted that her boyfriend is very controlling and only "allows" her to talk to certain people.

You Want to be the Perfect Wife

If you didn't start the give-away in the dating phase, you may have made the mistake of giving up and giving in in order to be the "perfect wife." My generation was brought up on television sitcoms that showed the dutiful wife hiding purchases or money spent on herself from the spouse, or rushing home to make sure the house was clean and supper was on the table for the Prince. Most of us start out wanting to be the perfect wife, which is fine as long as it doesn't mean giving up our true selves in the process. Unfortunately, too many women begin patterns of true codependence in this early phase of marriage, worrying too much about their husband's reactions to things and not enough about what is right for them. Deciding my every move based on how I think my husband will react, and not on my own feelings and knowledge, will lead me to lose my true self.

I walk a thin line here between "self" and "other" directed behavior (which we'll talk more about in the next chapter), implying that we need not be *self-centered*, but *self-caring*. There is a clear difference. In the first months and years of marriage, too many women get caught in this pattern of pleasing their husbands at the expense of meeting their own needs. This expense isn't counted in dollars, but counted in pieces of self that are given up each time we change the behavior, feelings, thoughts, or beliefs that are the real us. We may do these things just to please him, hoping to be the perfect wife. We mean well, but the outcome is deadly to the true self.

I counseled Alicia, a young bride who told me her new husband goes to topless bars and pays for lap dances. When she complained, he told her that she has a confidence problem and that these activities have nothing to do with her. She felt in her gut that it wasn't right, but she didn't want to upset her new husband. She came to me, uncertain as to whether something was wrong with her for feeling extremely uncomfortable about this situation. Through counseling she was able to have her feelings validated, something that friends or family could have done, but she didn't want family and friends to know about her husband's behavior. I gave this young bride a lot of credit for seeking out validation for her true feelings rather than just accepting what her husband was telling her. I encouraged her to know and trust her own voice.

In these first years of marriage the aspiring "perfect wife" may also begin other patterns of behavior that she will later regret. This is when young women start picking up and cleaning up after husbands who then don't feel responsible for cleaning up after themselves. The perfect wife "wannabe" may dash home from work to prepare a gourmet meal and wow her new husband, who may then come to expect it.

Trying to impress your man with your cooking or housekeeping skills isn't dangerous, but it may wear you out. The more dangerous pattern begins when young brides give in and give up their deeply held inner knowledge or values in order to please their husbands. Fear of abandonment doesn't decrease after the vows are spoken (as many assume), it increases after marriage, and even more after babies come along.

You're a Mommy Now

Some women manage to maintain their individualism early in the relationship, but see it slip away after they gave up their jobs or careers in order to have babies and stay home with the kids. Their confidence fades as they lack adult feedback and tangible rewards for their efforts. So many women say that they feel uninteresting, unattractive, and boring after staying home with kids for a few years. If I'm feeling that poorly about myself, then I probably will lack the confidence to stand up for myself or hold the line when someone tries to step over my boundaries. The reality is that women are more vulnerable when they are housewives and have no income of their own or have no consistent feedback about their worth (tangible or intangible). This contributes to a perceived loss of power and an increased fear of abandonment.

It is this lack of confidence and fear of abandonment that causes women to allow someone else's ideas, feelings, or desires to override their own. If women feel "less than" when not employed and producing dollars (even if they are treated that way), then they may begin participating in more "giving-up and giving-in" behaviors. Josie, a client who was a stay-at-home mom, told me how guilty she felt about asking for anything, but then she'd see her husband spend $800 on a golf weekend. She kept up a large house, did laundry for five people, cooked almost every day, and provided childcare for three children. Yet she couldn't buy a pair of shoes without guilt. After ten years of staying home with children, she felt unworthy even of necessities.

If we don't see our own worth, then our behavior will reflect that. Others can't make us feel guilt. Our feelings come from our own belief that we are doing something wrong. No matter how mad you get about my behavior, I won't feel guilt (anger maybe) unless I believe I've done something wrong. Check your beliefs.

I can't say enough about the negative effect that little or no adult feedback has on women who stay home all day with children. Children (immature by nature) scream at us when we are doing the right thing. When we say "no" to something that is bad or dangerous for them, they tell us they hate us, or make a public spectacle to embarrass us. When we spend an hour cleaning the living area, they trash it so that it looks untouched by the time your husband comes home from work. Now, he has been in a neat office all day, undisturbed by milk spills and tantrums. His co-workers and boss might even tell him when he's done a good job, and nobody undoes his job after he has spent hours getting it just right. He goes to the toilet and there's no one beating on the door and crying to get in. He has a lunch break where he goes to a nice restaurant and chit chats with intelligent people who don't throw their peas or spill chocolate milk into his lap.

Most women just don't get confidence boosts through childrearing and housekeeping activities; many of us go into the survival mode at best. These years are a vulnerable time when low confidence can prompt women to think that everybody in the world knows more than they do. Actually, the reason why women tend to be so much better at relationships than men is that they had to become experts while nurturing and educating young children who can be quite demanding at times.

Our fear of jeopardizing our marital relationship is greater when our kids are small and our responsibilities are big. Let's face it, we are even more afraid of abandonment when we have three hungry mouths to feed and we generate no income. We also allow ourselves to get very distracted during childrearing years, not a fault, but just the reality of this demanding period of life. We're preoccupied with the daily demands of childrearing and don't feel we have time to evaluate our own lives—what is working for us and what is not. We seem to jump from one "crisis" to the next. The energy that it takes to look beneath the surface is big, and extra energy isn't something we have a lot of during this laborious stage of life. We tend to put our own needs on the back burner as we focus on the kids and their issues. We're just more likely to focus on keeping the peace when we have the kids and a family unit to protect. Is this a good thing? Yes and no. Does it accomplish what we thought it would? Probably not. If we change ourselves for fear of disapproval or abandonment, we simply perpetuate a myth that isn't real. We also unwittingly teach our vulnerable children (particularly our female children) that a woman needs to give up her own likes, dislikes, needs and desires if they don't match her man's.

HOW DOES IT ACTUALLY HAPPEN... THE LOSS OF THE TRUE SELF?

Giving in to Keep the Peace

A young woman wants to talk to her sister and needs support because she is feeling down. Her husband tells her that she should keep her problems to herself, "It's nobody else's business, and anyway, you'll sound like a whiner; no one wants to hear it." She knows in her gut that her sister cares about her and wouldn't consider her sharing of feelings as whining. She lets his voice override her own voice because she doesn't want to upset the peace. Then she starts to doubt her feelings as *his* words penetrate her very thin layer of confidence. She walks away from the phone, again, and over time her relationship with her sister becomes more distant. However, resentment starts to build, and this creeping resentment starts to change how the young woman feels about her partner. *She* is the one that gave in on what she really wanted, needed, felt, or believed, but now she resents *him*. Not only does she get resentment instead of the "happy ever after," but he also gets cheated. Because she is doing or saying what he wants, he is initially rewarded. A little further down the road, however, he will notice that she is not so enamored with him anymore; she's now acting rather distant.

So you're young, charmed, and in love, and you want to change this one thing to keep him happy, or perhaps, just to keep the peace. But then you find that just this one change wasn't enough, and low and behold, the prince is only happy for brief moments, and all at your expense. You find yourself increasingly resentful, but you clam up when you feel the urge to put your foot down or "just say no" when asked to please him yet one more time. You don't want to upset the one who holds the key to your forever happiness, and besides, you think you can't stand conflict. You're afraid he'll be unhappy with you if you don't agree or give in, so you back down. You can see the never-ending loop that you're caught in. You do get moments of joy and you share some really good times, so you convince yourself it's worth the sacrifice. You must keep the peace...and thus begins the sacrifice of self.

A lot of women tell me they give in to the men in their lives simply to keep the peace. Carol, a woman that I'm seeing for panic disorder, had a friend drive her to her therapy session the other day. I asked her why she hadn't driven herself, thinking that perhaps her anxiety had worsened. Carol replied, "I had to get someone to bring me because George gets mad if I use his truck." "So what?" I asked. She looked bewildered. She explained that he would fuss and carry on if she asked to use his truck. Why does it take us so long to figure out that what we do in response to someone's actions is teaching that person how to treat us? This woman has unwittingly taught her husband this: if he makes a big enough fuss, she won't demand anything from him, not even the use of his truck while he's sleeping.

"THE LOOK"

Many women tell me that they gave up something they really needed (some time away from the kids, etc.) because of their husband's mild facial show of disapproval. "Did he threaten to beat you?" I'd asked. "No, he just made "that face." I'll admit when I was younger I gave in a thousand times because of "the look." But now "the look" doesn't faze me (except for an occasional thought about his face becoming stuck that way). Did the look change? No, I changed. So what happened, and how does the enlightened woman seem to grow beyond this kind of reactivity? In Chapter three I will tell you exactly how it's done—how to quit being over reactive and how to get back to being the real you.

For some women, "the look" is reserved mainly for public situations where her partner doesn't want to voice his disapproval out loud for others to hear. It's like being pinched under the table by your mother when you asked her Sunday dinner guest why she has a mustache. Of course you were six then, but now at thirty-six you expect to be able to judge for yourself what you should or shouldn't say. "The look" can also be used to stop you dead in your tracks in front of the children. The children see it as well as you, and they know that you are being chastised and therefore must have done something wrong. (It puts you on the same level as the kids and robs you of their respect.)

Danielle told me that her husband did not share her faith in God, and when she would try to say a blessing at the table at dinnertime her husband would give her "the look." The kids, of course, saw it as well as she did, and became conditioned to tense up anytime she would say the blessing. Finally, when she confronted him about his conveyance of disapproval, he was able to act more respectfully (and more maturely). She wished that she would have demanded that respect earlier, before the children learned to associate an unpleasant feeling with saying a blessing over food.

The Mini-Tantrum

Other behaviors, less subtle, can trigger women to give up and give in to things that aren't right for them. Many grown men throw mini-tantrums when their wives dare to say or do something for which they disapprove. I had Sally, a forty-three year-old woman in therapy, tell me that her husband screamed and yelled at her if she spent a few dollars over the weekly budget that he allotted her. (They were quite well to do and he spared no expense for himself.)This woman didn't have a spending problem and had rational reasons why her expenses would go over budget occasionally. She reacted to these tantrums by hiding things from her husband, which over time created much resentment towards him. She reacted to his bad behavior by hiding things, acting as if she had done something wrong when she *knew* she hadn't.

Some women enable two-year-old tantrum behavior in men. Alisha told me that her husband lies and cheats on her repeatedly. "Don't you confront him?" I asked. "I try, but he gets furious and screams and throws things and hits the wall," she replied. When he throws a tantrum, she shuts up. She has unwittingly taught him that she won't question his bad behavior if he throws a good tantrum. By giving up and giving in, she has enabled the very behavior that she hates to continue.

Pouting

Women may also react to pouting in the same way they react to "the look" or to tantrums by their partners. Robin told me that her husband doesn't want her to go to church, and he pouts all day Sunday if she goes anyway. She often reacts to the pouting by staying home to keep the peace, but then she feels guilty because in her gut she knows that going to church is right for her. She also began to resent his pouting because it made her give up something she really wanted and needed.

Women think they'll be happy if they keep the peace by giving up and giving in, and men think they'll be pleased and happy if women do what they want. The fact is that neither ends up being happy. The "victory" that he thinks he has won has changed the person that he originally loved, and this "forced" change causes her resentment and hostility that eventually takes over the relationship.

But aren't we supposed to have "give" as well as "take" in relationships? Isn't that what relationships are all about? You bet, but I'm looking at the big picture here. Women are much more likely to give up parts of their true selves in hopes of gaining approval. Men have society's approval to please themselves, and women are programmed by society to do what pleases men. Remember, giving of yourself is good; giving away yourself is bad.

QUESTIONS AND SUGGESTIONS

Question: In your primary relationship, have you been strong enough to assert your real knowledge, beliefs, values, needs, and desires for purpose? Has your behavior matched your inner knowledge?
Suggestion: If the answer is "no," make a list of your actions that do not match what you know, believe, or feel. For instance, are you allowing the children to watch "R" rated movies because your husband says it's okay, even though it goes against everything you know and believe about what is right? Identify the specific behavior on your part that enables this thing that you believe is wrong to happen. Write down a new behavior that asserts your beliefs and sets a clear boundary. As in the previous example, talk to your husband in private about what you think and how you feel when your small children are exposed to "R" rated movies. Then tell him exactly how you need for him to behave when they want to watch these movies. Tell him that you need for him to support your strong belief and knowledge that this is bad for young children.

Question: Can you identify any area where you have built up resentment toward your partner?
Suggestion: If you have resentment, then you probably have repeatedly given up and given in when you knew, believed, or felt strongly about something. Try to pinpoint one behavior that you resent on the part of your partner. For example, you may resent your partner for going to play golf four times a week. Now imagine another wife setting boundaries with her husband, asserting her need for assistance with the children or chores, and not tolerating four golf games a week. Write down what you think she says and does to get this need met.

Question: Are you familiar and comfortable with the person you see staring back at you from the mirror or have you turned into a stranger?

Suggestion: List qualities or behaviors that you see in yourself that you know are not a reflection of the "real you. " "I used to be ______, but now I'm _______. From the "I used to be" list, identify the behaviors or attitudes that you would like to "reincorporate" into your life. Now write down one thing that you can do that would start you on the path to becoming that way again. For instance, if you used to be "fun," write down one fun thing that you could do. If you used to be "adventurous," write down an adventurous activity you'd like to do. Now, go out and do it!

3 Have a Midlife Crisis—Lord Knows you Need One!

It often takes a crisis to wake us up to reality; in this case, the reality is that we have been giving away little pieces of our true self for years. I used to cringe when I heard the words *midlife crisis.* Those words summoned images of balding men with pot bellies wearing halfway buttoned shirts. Not a pretty sight. I really feared the big midlife crisis, since time after time in my therapist chair I heard middle-aged husbands tell their wives how they have found other love interests (usually twenty years younger) and will be moving out next week. I used to feel sorry for the stunned wife who seemed so bewildered and lost. But my thoughts and feelings about midlife and the dreaded *crisis* have taken a drastic turn, and I'll tell you why.

If you look up the word "crisis" in the dictionary you'll find that there is a very positive choice among the many meanings listed. A "crisis" indicates a turning point. Optimistically, this provides us with a chance to evaluate what's not working, and a chance to do something different. I always tell a client in crisis that this can be a window of opportunity, a chance to take a better path. When a person is in crisis, she is flexible, off balance, and more easily able to bend and turn in another direction. When things are plodding along as usual (no matter how badly), we are fixed and pretty set in our ways. It's only in a good crisis that we can break loose and change—hopefully for the better. At midlife women are becoming more reflective and more introspective, which is a fertile atmosphere for change. Our new insights not only may help us change, but may help us come to accept the things that we can't change at this stage of our lives. Today, many women in midlife are making exciting changes, learning how and when to be more accepting, how to have clearer boundaries, and how to rediscover and be true to themselves. They are furthering their education, finding careers, choosing to stay home, changing careers, and gaining assertiveness and confidence. Best of all, they are getting back in touch with themselves, their true selves, after years of focusing on others.

MIDLIFE CRISIS FORMALLY DEFINED

Most researchers place midlife somewhere between age forty and sixty and lasting about fifteen years. Don't panic, you're not expected to be in crisis for those fifteen years! Unfortunately, most of our attention has gone into studies and research on childhood, adolescence, and old age, leaving midlife as the stage of life least formally studied. Part of the reason midlife has been dreaded by so many is because almost everything written about it paints a picture of endings, loss, and the start of a downhill slope. Our society certainly doesn't value the elderly, and at mid-life we know we'll soon be in that "elderly" category. We all, however, seem to know women who appear to grow more creative and productive through those midlife years.

There are a lot of different factors that determine if you will have a "crisis" at midlife and just how severe it will be. The kind of resources that a woman has to pull from, including the quality of her marriage or other significant relationships, her educational and economic status, and her physical, emotional, and mental health, will all impact how she navigates her midlife transition.

Most women are trying to deal with the physical and emotional symptoms of menopause or peri-menopause at the same time that they are starting to examine and question everything in their lives. Also, the roles for males and females in our society have undergone a drastic change, and we as a generation are paving a new road with unclear guidelines and expectations. If you think about it, our mothers didn't have the choices and the ability to take control over their lives in the way that we have. Most weren't prepared to enter the work force and many never considered it. My mother's midlife crisis displayed a lot of mood changes and tears, while mine involved taking a graduate degree, restarting a career, road trips to adventurous places, and pajama parties with women friends!

Best Place to Be?

Recently, a large research project by the John D. and Catherine T. MacAuthur Foundation Research Network on Successful Midlife Development revealed a different picture of the middle years as the "best place to be." Their findings agree with my own experience, as well as my experience in counseling women: Midlife is a time when people can experience increased control over their lives and begin a journey of personal growth. I often see women in midlife move from dependence to independence, taking control over their own lives, sometimes for the first time. In their younger years many went from being under the control of parents to being controlled by a spouse and have never experienced the freedom to call their own shots, or choose their own directions. They lacked the needed confidence, were usually tied down with young children, and often didn't have the support of spouses to pursue their own dreams.

I was shocked the other day when a fifty-something friend revealed to me that her husband used to tell her what she could wear as well as when and where she could go. She admitted that she allowed it because she was afraid of his reaction. "He wasn't violent or anything, I just didn't want to make him mad." But this was before midlife, before she furthered her education and became employed in a professional job. It's ever so clear to me why men have not wanted women to have the same educational or financial advantages throughout history. What would marriage look like if every woman was secure financially and the partnership started out with each having equal money and/or earning potential?

In my forties I made the decision to return to higher education to seek a graduate degree. It was the beginning of new choices and directions toward self discovery and personal growth. Women today are challenging an old myth that says by midlife we have accomplished all that we are going to accomplish. Today women in their late thirties, forties, and fifties are rediscovering selves, finding the time and energy to start new pursuits and taking off in new directions. We are more aware than ever before about the need to be true to ourselves, to reach out to friends, and to seek balance in our lives.

WHAT TRIGGERS THE CRISIS IN THE FIRST PLACE?
Loss and Change

Some midlife crises may be triggered by a sudden change or life crisis such as a death of a parent, the loss of a job, or an extra-marital affair. For some women it is the anticipation of the last child leaving home that throws them off balance and cues them to begin examining their place in life. As long as there were kids at home their purpose was clear, but now, even though they may be able to stay busy with tasks, there is no longer a clear goal or sense of purpose. For women, a crisis appears to be triggered more from loss or changes in relationships, whereas for men it is more likely to be about job or career, or loss of physical ability. Women who have focused too much on their children and not enough on their spouses or friendships will be more shaken when their last child moves out of their homes. Those who become enmeshed with their children to the exclusion of friendships and partnerships with spouses have not only set themselves up for a rocky life transition into middle age, but they are often setting their children up for trouble and dysfunction as they struggle to separate and move on. I frequently see college-age women who have been their mother's "best friend" and are now struggling with symptoms of anxiety or depression as they experience guilt over their mother's loneliness. Women who have healthy relationships with children (they parent them, not befriend them), healthy relationships with spouses (they are partners, not inferiors), and healthy relationships with other women will have a more positive midlife transition. The unhealthier a woman is relationally, the more likely she is to experience the "midlife crisis" in a negative way.

But there isn't always a defining moment or event that triggers a woman to begin reflecting, examining, and evaluating her life up to that point. Some people's lives are considerably calmer in the middle years as opposed to the earlier years when they were finding jobs, getting married, taking care of small children, or buying first houses. With these demands behind them, some women may actually feel more secure and settled with their finances, and without childcare concerns they can experience more freedom to do more things for themselves. These life changes actually enable women to look to their midlife turning points as times to be anticipated and not to be dreaded.

Another change over time is that women are now having children at later ages than they did fifty years ago. This creates an interesting dilemma; you're ready to "move on" and focus on yourself, but you also want to support your children by attending soccer games and going to parent/teacher conferences. At forty-two I had a two-year-old, but I felt that I couldn't wait another minute to go back and finish my graduate degree. I had taken about ten years off from full-time outside employment to stay home with my children, and I had watched my colleagues move ahead in accomplishments and experience. There wasn't any one event that sparked this "crisis" point, just a building up of frustration and restlessness. Thus began the most definable turning point in my midlife journey—returning to school.

Actually, there was an earlier "awakening" at the age of thirty-four that was triggered by one of those classic life crises. I became aware that my husband was overly involved in a friendship with a younger woman and, after becoming angry and hurt, I began my first real change of life. I began to be assertive—setting clear boundaries, saying how I really felt, and saying what I really wanted. This often requires the removal, or the threat of removal, of the "safety net." By the term "safety net," I am referring to that false assurance and security that women have when they erroneously believe that a man will always be there to provide and take care of them. That was a fairy tale. I realized that the net could collapse at any time and I best stop feeling numb and unable to react and take control of my own life.

Women who wait until their late thirties or early forties to have children may postpone their midlife "crisis" until they are in their early fifties. Again, if the main relationships in their lives are going along smoothly, they may cruise a bit longer before they feel the need for change. For a woman who continues working when she has children, there may be no sense of loss (no given-up career) and less change until the last child leaves home. And, again, if she has invested in a good marriage and friendships and has outside interests and ambitions, there may be no "crisis" at all.

"Oh My God, My Life is Half Over!"

You've read books about midlife crises or perhaps you've seen it happen; we panic when something, for whatever reason, causes us to realize that our life is half over. But the questions triggered by this realization can be quite different for men than for women. Men may ask, "What *else* do I want to do with my life?" Women may be asking, "What can I *begin* to do with my life?" Men have generally been able to be more focused on themselves, their own careers, and their own success. Many women have had to, or chosen to, put off their own education, career pursuits, or personal success for the sake of the kids, or sometimes so the husband can pursue his goals. I think we all can agree that women's lives change more than men's after marriage and even more so after children are born.

More women than men are likely to rearrange jobs, quit jobs, and as mentioned earlier, take on most of the housekeeping chores. They are the ones who are more likely to stay home on Saturday to watch the kids while dad plays golf. And after all, he has been "working" all week and you haven't. He would just have to announce, "I have a golf game tomorrow at 1:00," and it would happen. You, on the other hand, had to spend hours on the phone looking for a sitter if you wanted to go out with a friend. Therefore, you likely became gradually more and more disconnected from friends, and further and further away from your old activities that you did for enjoyment. Women have also typically given a lot of their "free" time to the neighborhood, school, scout, or church activities of their children. Midlife women have more of what psychologist David M. Almieda, PhD, calls "crossover" stressors. By this he means that women, more than men, tend to shoulder simultaneous responsibilities like work, family, church, and community, and report higher levels of distress as a result.

Men are also more likely to continue their usual "play" activities than women after children are born. Many are likely to continue golfing, fishing, or playing sports with the guys. Women are spending more time with the kids and are more likely to become lonely by midlife. I've heard so many women say that trying to have lunch with friends with kids interrupting every minute isn't worth it to them, so they've given up trying. They not only gave up peer relationships from work, but now may slip further and further away from friends and even family as they assume caretaking responsibility for children, house, and husband. When this happens, the female midlife crisis is set apart from that of the male's, as the "self" they once knew can be a bit harder to find. I've heard so many women say, "I feel like a dummy after washing dishes and doing laundry for fifteen years. Who in the world would find me interesting?" They view themselves as "less than" since our society has not put a high value on homemaking or childcare. Homemakers earn zero dollars and childcare workers make minimum wage. Modern society has put its greatest value on that which produces the almighty dollar, not the home, and certainly not powerless, penniless children. Therefore many women, having had less opportunities to pursue their own purpose, careers, or dreams, are likely to try to attain these things when they recognize that, indeed, their lives are half over.

Can You Actually Plan for a Crisis?

Today, some women actually do plan for their midlife "crises. "They might start taking classes while their kids are still in school, with the goal of going back to work when the eldest ones get into high school or graduate. They may start part-time jobs with the hope of later moving into full-time. Some women (in anticipation of empty nests) begin researching career possibilities by talking to counselors or advisors at the local college or university, or taking aptitude tests which are offered at some colleges or facilities.

In the same period men are usually well established in their careers and may not anticipate the need for planning and are more likely caught off guard by the midlife urges for change. Some women feel more trapped during the years of childrearing while men typically have more space to move about in career pursuits and leisure activities. The reverse happens around midlife when men feel trapped by their long established careers and women are suddenly freed as the kids move out of the home. Women can now do what men did earlier—seek education, careers, or more leisure activities. When my children were young it seemed I was always standing in the door holding a little one while my husband was waving goodbye as he left for some sport or social activity. Now, I seem to be the one waving goodbye as I toodle off with my women friends after he comes home exhausted from a long, hard day at the office.

The Questions We Ask

In midlife crisis men seem to be asking, "Am I still attractive? Am I still virile? Am I still physically strong?" Women experiencing that crisis seem to be asking, "Who the heck am I? What is my worth? What is my purpose?" Men are asking themselves if they are still powerful; women are often just discovering that they have any power at all. "Who will I be now that I don't have to invest all of my time and energy in our home and children?" Men are asking, "What else can I accomplish for myself?" Many women are asking, "What can I begin to accomplish for me?" Most men are probably in the same career that they would have been in had they not had children. Most men never gave up a promotion or cut back to part time because of the children. As a result, however, they may have been so dedicated to their jobs that a crisis can arise when they realize that they have missed out on intimate family relationships and events because of time spent at work.

We can't discount that the midlife event has changed over time more for women than for men. Men's roles haven't changed as much as women's have in the last century. Birth control and new opportunities in the workplace have revolutionized life for women. We have more choices outside the home and don't feel as trapped or limited when we become restless and feel the need for change in midlife. I don't know about you, but I've noticed fewer women moaning about an empty nest in the last few years. Some women are actually jumping up and down for joy when that last kid finally leaves home!

One of my friends is looking forward to taking on new challenges after her son leaves for college this fall. Her life is so full that she actually had to put the brakes on so she could "mother" him these last few months. Because more women today are working outside the home, or are involving themselves in multiple activities outside the home, they are less affected by empty houses. Women in their forties and fifties are more ready to help children grow independent because they are connected with colleagues and women friends; they have lives of their own apart from their children.

Nonetheless, both men and women seem off balance during this "crisis" period of life. Even if the questions are different, both are questioning themselves and looking for a kind of affirmation as in "Tell me I'm okay." The definition of "okay" is different for each of us. Some are asking, "What have I missed out on?" or "Am I being who I want to be?" or "Am I doing what I want to be doing?" Even with our differences, it seems that some of the questions men and women ask aren't really all that far apart; we both feel we've missed out on something. However, the way we go about searching for the answers can be very different.

THE MIDLIFE STEREOTYPES

You all know the stereotypes when referring to a man's midlife crisis. He has an affair with a twenty-five-year old and/or buys a motorcycle or a fast sports car. He might also act out by spiking his hair or wearing his shirt half open with a gold chain showing underneath. Instead of calling a male friend for lunch to talk over his troubles at the office, this stereotype may start sharing his woes with the secretary. Before you know it he's having an affair. Let's face it; having sex is easier than having a real friendship. Now I know these are stereotypes, and all men don't act in these ways, but enough do in order to have created "stereotypical behavior." Several of my parents' friends went through marital upheavals when their husbands had affairs. But every one of the wives stayed in the marriages because most had no resources and felt trapped. They had never worked outside the home, had no college educations, training, or abilities to support themselves; they just became depressed. This is just more evidence that education is the key to real progress for women.

"They're Acting Like Adolescents"

When men chase younger women and buy themselves sports cars at midlife, we say they are acting like "adolescents." And what did adolescent boys do? They chased girls and cruised around attempting to impress them with fast, powerful vehicles. They tried to impress, create an image, one that was very different from whom they really were. They were sometimes dishonest with other males in order to uphold the "image" of the virile conqueror. They weren't likely to share their vulnerabilities with their buddies. The stories told in the locker room weren't exactly accurate, and no one wanted his buddy to find out that he didn't actually score last night.

Is there a stereotype that immediately comes to mind when referring to a woman's midlife crisis? No, not really. I guess men do have a stereotype for women midlifers; the words "hormonal" and "menopausal" come to mind. Few women go looking for powerful sports cars and few women leave their families to move in with men twenty years their junior. Yes, the re-evaluation of our life at that point may make us a little crabby, but instead of worrying about "image" so much during the midlife crisis, more women seem to be searching for something real, their "real" selves. They want to look beyond the *roles* they have played—mothers, wives, or housekeepers. "If I wasn't someone's wife, who would I be? If I wasn't someone's mother, who would I be?" Women don't usually seek these answers from men; they turn to other women, friends, or family.

We Can Act Like Adolescents Too

Although it really does seem on the surface that there are very few things in common in the male and female midlife crisis, there is at least one common element. Like men, some women today are behaving like adolescents during their midlife crises. And what were adolescent girls like? How did they behave? They were hanging out with girlfriends, having sleepovers, laughing together, crying together, and giving each other emotional support through the traumas of relationships with boys, hormonal upheaval, and trouble with parents. They listened to feedback from girlfriends, sometimes more than they listened to family. Nothing was as important as their friends. They told their girlfriends their secrets, they stayed up talking half the night, and they did everything together. They showed their vulnerabilities more than their male counterparts and got support in return. The view of self that they struggled for was less an "image" than an accurate reflection. Since more truths were shared, feedback was more honest and accurate. As girls, we were also with our friends for several hours a day, as opposed to the few minutes that we share when we get into adulthood.

During adolescence, we focused on ourselves and our friends. But from college on, we spent less and less time with friends as dating, marriage, and children took priority. By the time we were in the young adult stages of life, most of us were dating seriously or marrying and doing "our" thing, and none or very little of "my thing." But in midlife this all begins to change back, back to more "me" with a decreased focus on "we."

Midlife and adolescence have in common a focus on peer relationships, new experiences, fun, and self-exploration. Also, like adolescents, our bodies are changing. Our hormones are giving us grief just like when we were teens; we may even be moody and snap at our families like we did then.

SAME SEX FEEDBACK

Some men tend to seek feedback and validation from the opposite sex during midlife (therefore the need to attract that twenty-five-year-old to verify virility), whereas women tend to return to their pursuit of same-sex feedback. The man at midlife who looks to his young girlfriend in order to "find himself" is in for a real letdown. The view a woman gets of her self from another woman is more accurate because it is not sexualized or romanticized. If women seek their support from other women at midlife, and if they are being more open and honest when talking to other women, then the feedback they receive has to reflect back a more accurate image of their self. You can see immediately why this same-sex support might be a bit healthier and less harmful to others! It's when men or women turn to the opposite sex during midlife that havoc is likely wrought on the self, the marriage, and the family.

All over the country, groups of midlife women are seeking same-sex feedback as they gather for social, spiritual, or educational purposes. Women are searching for and creating new opportunities to bond with other women. It is changing the way women experience their midlife crisis. We'll talk more about our need and search for "girlfriends" in Chapter Five.

This grouping of women may have been happening earlier to some extent, but not nearly as much as today. In very early times when the whole extended family lived in the same place, women had their "natural groups" and therefore their built-in support. Then after the industrial age, families became more mobile, and more and more women raised their children and experienced the empty nest without their family there for support. Tied to the house, women became increasingly isolated, and you can see what kind of crisis might occur when kids leave home.

The new midlife crisis is easier to handle because women (who aren't family) are grouping up to support each other when they begin this major life transition. They can share their experiences and laugh about their sagging breasts while sipping margaritas. I am currently having wonderful times with my women friends and, unlike the male stereotype, the last thing in the world that I want is to have a relationship with another person of the opposite sex. (One is plenty, thank you very much.) There is nothing but trouble looming for those women who start sharing their problems and crying on the shoulder of some man at the office. Before long they are involved in affairs and have ten times the problems they had in the beginning. If they had sought out some women friends to share their feelings and thoughts, they might have gotten some practical help and been able to actually clear up some problems instead of creating new ones!

THE NEW FOCUS—YOU

Women notoriously feel uncomfortable when they start thinking about doing something for themselves. Most often their comfort zone is really in doing for others, and they will often spend their therapy hour talking about others, resulting in less help for themselves. Don't get me wrong; doing for others is good and right, but let me clarify one thing here. As mentioned earlier, there is a clear difference between being self-centered and self-caring. I often see women in therapy who don't know how to be self-caring, and as a result, they get themselves into all kind of messes. Because of their focus on what is good for others, and not themselves, they allow others to treat them in ways that might be totally contrary to what is in their best interest.

This inability to take care of themselves leads to gradual erosion of their true selves or, at best, losses in some pieces of these selves.

For instance, the woman who gives up the art class she wanted to take (just because her husband thinks it's a waste of time) may lose the creative piece of herself if she keeps giving up and giving in over time. The woman who does not focus on her own needs (balancing hers with others' needs) will likely not develop her own gifts and talents and will likely feel inadequate, less than. The woman who knows how to give, but knows how to say "no" when she needs time to refresh herself, educate herself, nurture her interests, or renew her spirit, will have a more balanced and satisfying life experience.

Women who give and give and never say "no" present themselves in therapy as depressed and resentful. They are often afraid of the consequences of saying "no," fearing that they can't handle others being unhappy with them. They haven't learned that it is okay to take care of themselves and that they can do it without being selfish. Having difficulty setting boundaries and allowing people to run all over you isn't the same as being a "giving" person who cheerfully helps meet the needs of others. If you see these bad habits in yourself, you may need professional help in learning how to set clear boundaries so that you can do what you need to do to take care of yourself and change for the better. Remember, too much giving, and no renewing or self preservation, will leave you an empty vessel.

That Old Feeling—Guilt!

Women who see themselves as "caretakers" may experience more guilt and internal conflict when midlife desires for change and the desire to focus on themselves hits. Those who learned how to take care of themselves when younger are less likely to experience guilt during the midlife crisis. Taking care of yourself in not a "me first" attitude; it's a "me too" attitude. If you don't act like you matter, neither will others. Getting your needs met leads to happiness; take responsibility for your own happiness!

Meg, a client, had put everybody else first, never taking time for herself to meet her own needs. She had few, if any, friends because she was never available to spend time with others. She had put her education on hold so that her husband wouldn't be inconvenienced. She didn't want to upset her husband, so she never demanded that he come straight home after work or share in the housekeeping or childcare responsibilities. In other words, she was that giver who never stops giving, taking nothing for herself. Then one day she learned that her husband was having an affair with a twenty-seven-year-old woman. Not only had she unwittingly enabled his affair by not setting boundaries, but she had also failed to prepare herself should her "safety net" fail. Her self esteem was low since she had not put time or energy into giving herself the things she needed. As a therapist, I could see that she had set herself up for this crisis by not being true to herself, clinging to a false belief that if she kept everyone else happy, she'd find happiness and safety. In the short term she made her husband happy by not setting boundaries or demanding that he participate more in family care activities, but in the long run she set herself up to be used and abused.

Why do so many younger women feel guilty when they do things for themselves? Well, your feelings come from the meanings that you put on things. Guilt comes from believing that something you've done is "wrong" or something you have is undeserved. Why and where did women get the belief that doing for themselves or having for themselves is wrong? Why do we feel okay about pleasing our partner but not okay about doing what pleases us? Perhaps patriarchy, men's tales, society's tales, and the fairy tales have convinced us that because we are "less than," we don't deserve the same attention to our own needs.

When I was younger my husband used to tell me what he had planned and I used to "ask" him before I planned anything. He would tell me when he was going out of town to run in a race, or going somewhere with a friend, and I would adjust my schedule or give up whatever I had to in order to be there with our children. If I wanted to go somewhere, I didn't feel that I could just announce it like he did, but felt I had to check with him for his convenience. I often felt guilty if he looked perturbed by my plans. There was definitely a double standard into which I played.

Nobody *made* me feel guilty. But because I was staying home with a child and cleaning house, I didn't *feel* as important or valued, and therefore I didn't expect the same courtesy and consideration from my husband as he did from me. My beliefs affected my feelings, and my behavior reflected my thoughts and feelings. It was my behavior that enabled him to behave the way that he did, and I had to take responsibility for that before it could change. Now, I expect equal consideration; now I behave in ways that do not enable inconsiderate treatment.

Taking Care of Yourself During Menopause

A number of experts and a ton of books guide us through this part of our midlife crisis, particularly the physical part. One doctor tells you to take hormones and then you come home and watch the news only to hear something about their horrible dangers. Today, more women are taking responsibility for their own health during this time of physical and emotional change. They are reading a variety of reports, talking to other women, and trying more than "what the doctor ordered." I know some women who forgo the pills (even though their doctors immediately tried to pop them on hormones), and I know some who are trying and feeling better after natural remedies and less conventional approaches. Fewer women today are allowing drug companies to dictate what they should or should not do about the natural changes of menopause. Some menopausal women still choose conventional pharmaceutical remedies to alleviate unpleasant symptoms, but the difference is that more are knowledgeably choosing, not passively accepting, this as the only way to alleviate discomfort.

I wonder if we don't over treat menopausal women. I know some women have horrible hot flashes or other nasty symptoms that need to be treated medically, but it seems (and recent research confirms) that we leave women on hormones too long…even after the symptoms have stopped. Some have no symptoms at all and doctors put them on hormones anyway. I had no symptoms and tried hormones at my doctor's recommendation. I immediately felt depressed and slightly homicidal. The majority of us are learning to navigate through menopause with some changes in our diet, exercise, and perhaps an increase in our calcium intake.

The good news is that once these menopausal symptoms pass, women get a new burst of energy, coined by Margaret Mead as "post-menopausal zest. "Gail Sheehy in *New Passages* reminds us that once a woman has come through menopause she can say goodbye to fears about pregnancy or monthly mood swings, and she isn't any longer confined by society's definition of her as a sex object or breeder. It is then that she can truly be all parts of herself and feel free to say what she really thinks. I believe we can get stuck in the discomfort of change or we can use this regained freedom to step out and expand ourselves. Wouldn't it be great if we could get back some of the gutsiness and belief in ourselves that we had as girls.

ROCKING THE BOAT AND FINDING YOU CAN SWIM

The midlife crisis is a time of restlessness, movement, and change, yet it's impossible to change course if I put all of my energy into keeping the boat stable, determined to navigate the same course. I can't take advantage of the crisis as a "turning point" if I'm afraid of shaking things up a bit. Many of us spend the vast majority of our time and energy in relationships avoiding conflict and avoiding actions that might rock the boat. What are we so afraid of? Falling out of the boat, I suppose, or more likely, afraid that *he'll* fall out. We're probably afraid to rock the boat because we lack confidence in our ability to navigate our own way.

Maybe you shouldn't be afraid to scream a little...jump up and down...rock the boat...but don't jump out...just find a better seat. Take hold of the stern, choose a new course, and start paddling, and if you need a little support, pick up the phone and call that friend you haven't spoken to in three months. To cope with the fear you may experience when shaking things up a bit, seek out some same-sex support. If you don't already have supportive females in your life, then figure out what you'll have to do to meet people like you and JUST DO IT. Women in midlife are discovering that they can rock the boat and not fall out...or lose any of the crew.

A midlife "crisis" seems shaky and off balance, but we must remember that it is in the shakiness that we are more able to break loose from our old ways and take better paths. However, even desired positive change will not occur without your willingness to rock the boat. In Chapter Four, I'll become more specific regarding what behavior changes are necessary to shake things up, allowing for positive change.

He May Not Like It...But He'll Adjust

How do men typically react to the woman's midlife crisis when the boat starts rocking? If a man typically begins questioning his own virility during midlife and typically validates it through attention from women, what must he be thinking when his partner shows signs of questioning her own value and searching for her own validation? You've got it! He may automatically fear that she is looking for the same thing that men are stereotypically looking for; he might assume that she needs and seeks validation from the opposite sex. He might become insecure at her signs of "branching out" for fear that she might be looking for his replacement. Her increased time away with "the girls" might frighten him. He might show resistance to her new quest for friends and might show disapproval of new ideas, such as furthering her education.

These changes could all be very threatening to someone who doesn't understand the female midlife "crisis." Her new response to "the look" (ignoring it) will serve to frighten him even more. She must remember that her key to success is to *not* react to his show of disapproval. We enable someone's control over us by giving in every time they show disapproval. Just stick to your guns and others will gradually adjust. Need I remind you, balance is the key. It's not all or nothing. Don't jump from "less than" to "all that"...take care of your self and your own needs in balance with your partner's and family's.

Change brings about the unknown, and the unknown creates anxiety. The male partner needs much reassurance that acquiring attention from the opposite sex is not what *your* changing is about. You must assure him that your focus is on yourself and that he will love you all the more when you've completed your journey. You might also remind him that you could be spending thousands of dollars on plastic surgery, but instead you have decided to work on your relationships with women friends, your spiritual growth, and your intellectual growth. He won't know whether to get down on his knees and thank you or run and hide under the bed!

QUESTIONS AND SUGGESTIONS

Question: What negative connotations and beliefs come to mind when you think about your current, past, or potential midlife crisis?
Suggestion: Take each belief about negative possibilities and write it down. Now, think about and write down at least one positive possibility for each negative one you listed. For example, if you listed as a negative belief, "It's a time of losses," you might write beside it, "I will gain more time for myself with the kids gone. I might take some classes and gain new skills. I have more time to cultivate friends. We can travel more often now."

Question: What resources do you have to help get you through a midlife crisis, turning point, or life transition?
Suggestion: Make a list of your resources such as: Marriage? Friendships? Family? Neighbors? Work? Faith? Fun? Physical Fitness? Intellectual stimulation? Now give each a quality rating from one to ten. Your lowest numbers will tell you where your priorities for work and attention may need to fall. For instance, if the quality of your family relationships is an "eight" and the quality of friendships is a "two," you might want to put more time into cultivating and nurturing friendships

Question: Do you experience a feeling of guilt when thinking of doing something just for yourself?
Suggestion: Think of the last thing that you did for yourself but then felt guilty about. Since our feelings come from the meanings we put on things, you will have to examine your beliefs about doing something for yourself. For instance, have you been telling yourself that you are "selfish" whenever you do something that is solely for you? Look up the word "selfish" in the dictionary. If that definition describes you, you probably don't need this book. Now, think of a more accurate meaning to put on your activity that was just for you. If you believe that it was "self caring," meeting a need for which you are responsible, your guilt will melt away. Example:You went out with a couple of girlfriends and laughed yourself silly last Tuesday night while your husband was home helping the kids with their homework and putting them to bed. He gave you "the look" and sighed loudly when you came home. You will feel guilty if you believe you did something wrong. You will not feel guilty if you believe that you are responsibly meeting your need to have fun in your life.

4 Retrieving the Lost Self—Reclaiming the Real You

Where Do I Begin?

So you've had your wake up call, you've faced that stranger staring blankly at you in the mirror, and you've been thrown into crisis as you both desire and fear change at the same time. You're torn between clinging to the familiar (no matter how bad it is) and taking risks by jumping into what seems like unknown territory. You might even get up the nerve to jump, but you don't have a clue what you'd jump into, so you may just become paralyzed with fear, moving neither forward nor backward. The discomfort you're experiencing is making you feel anxious and irritable and you're noticing every little irritating thing about the people around you.

Ginger, a forty-six-year-old woman, was referred to me by her physician after she went to see him asking for antidepressants. She described anxiety symptoms that seemed to be related to times that she was arguing with her husband. She went on to tell me things about her marriage that she has never told anyone before. "He drinks too much almost every night. He calls me 'fat ass,' and when we argue, he threatens to leave." When she told him that she was going to see a counselor he threatened to clean out their savings account. When I asked her if she had shared any of this with her friends or family, she said, "I would tell my family, but I'm afraid that they'll tell me to do something, and I'm not ready to leave." So many women fear that their only alternative to a miserable existence is to divorce their husbands. They equate "changing" with exiting the relationship completely. Many avoid counseling for this same reason; they fear the therapist will immediately tell them to leave their husbands. But most likely their counselor will help them focus on changing themselves *within* their marriage, and few usually have to leave in order to find themselves. They do, however, have to tolerate a little boat rocking and risk taking in order for positive change to occur. The fear of the relationship ending stops many women dead in their tracks, paralyzing them and preventing them from making any strides in personal growth. Certainly there are times when leaving is the only answer, but more often the fear of abandonment and marital breakup is unwarranted. Their focus may be on the wrong people… their partners.

Taking Responsibility
"If He'd Just Change"–Blaming the Right Person

The biggest mistake that women make after they wake up to face the loss of their real selves is to blame it on the people around them. Taking responsibility for where you are, how you feel, and where you will end up will make all the difference in the world in how you navigate your turning point. We talked earlier about the stereotypical behavior of midlife men, when instead of looking inside themselves during the misery of their "crisis," they look to younger women to boost their self image. We know, however, that their "fix" will be temporary; they have to face themselves eventually. If we blame others for our unhappiness, then we mistakenly expect that others can fix it and make us happy. Remember your original fantasy about Prince Charming? That's what got you into this pickle in the first place; you looked to someone else to make you happy. Now that the fairy tale failed, you make a second error by blaming him and being angry at him for not fixing it. He couldn't make you happy in the first place, so he surely can't fix your unhappiness now. Blaming him for your bad choices and lack of assertiveness won't serve to get you one bit closer to discovering your true self again.

I see some women who wake up to their misery and have the courage to see counselors, but then get stuck in the anger and blaming stage. They can suddenly see what's happened to them, but they focus on someone else's behavior as the problem. "If he would just...." Tammy, a beautiful forty-three-year-old woman married to someone who was her superior on an educational and financial level, came to see me in crisis as she was feeling split down the middle, miserable, but not wanting to break up her family. She described how her husband treated her like a child and kept her in the dark about finances (requiring that she justify every penny spent). He chose her friends, and made her account for every minute she was away from the house. She hadn't left him because she hoped that *he* would change. "What would motivate him to change?" I asked her. "I don't know," she answered. "How long have you been miserable?" I asked. "I've been unhappy for years," she said. "Has your being unhappy for years motivated him to behave differently, to change?" I asked. "No," she answered. "So, I guess if you keep doing the same thing, you can count on getting the same thing," I said. Then there was silence.

Wouldn't it be easier if everybody else would just change to suit us? Many of us aren't feeling better because we aren't *doing* better; we're waiting for someone else to do better...then we'll be happy. Well, get over it, because most people aren't going to do better until it's required of them. The only other thing that might motivate someone to do better is a higher "misery index." You know, you get so miserable that you're willing to get up off of your rear end and do something. In this case, the only thing that would motivate her husband to change would be if she changed. If her responses changed, then his old behavior would no longer work for him. If his old behavior no longer worked for him, he'd have to find a new way to behave. She unwittingly made his bad behaviors work successfully for him...motivating him to continue to do more of the same. Put simply, we keep doing what works. However, because she gave up and gave in, backing down time after time in order to keep the peace, it eventually changed who she was. Her behavior (based on his desires, not hers) gradually turned her into someone else, as we *behave* our way to *being*. The inner turmoil that she now feels is anything but peace. In the short haul her giving-in behavior prevented arguments, but in the long haul it created inner conflict and misery.

Becoming Intentional About Change

Your search for self must be intentional; you must be willing to focus on yourself with a specific purpose and direction in mind. Many women are thinking about everybody but themselves. They are intentional about taking care of their husband's needs and happiness; they are intentional about caring for their children and doing what they need to do to make them happy. A woman who has for years been giving up time with friends in order to help her children get their homework done might later find it difficult to meet with girlfriends and share a meal and good conversation. She's just not used to giving to herself; it doesn't feel right. A woman who has given in time after time in order to keep her husband from getting ticked off and pouting will definitely have a hard time focusing on her own needs and standing up for herself

Many women have focused on others' needs for so long that they literally don't know what their own needs are anymore. These women find it very difficult to change the focus to themselves in midlife. In other words, it won't come naturally; they must be intentional about identifying and meeting their own needs. They may need help in remembering what used to be important to them, how they used to have fun, or what they used to want more than anything in the world. Opening up to your friends and family about your current loss of self can open the door to rediscovering who you used to be.

Once a woman can be intentional about her focus and behavior (recognizing the behaviors that aren't helping her) and stop blaming others (taking responsibility for her own behavior choices), she'll be well on her way to rediscovering her true self. The first step to authenticity is to take responsibility for where you are and to become intentional about changing the things that *you* do that aren't getting you what you want. These changes in *thinking* have to happen before you're ready to make changes in your *behavior*.

Changing Your Behavior
Quit Backing Down

Tammy's husband behaved inappropriately and then put her down if she complained about it. "He always turned it around to me, and I would end up feeling like such a dummy before it's all over." He flirted openly with other women at social gatherings, but when she confronted him about it he would tell her that she just had a jealously problem and didn't feel secure about herself. When I asked Tammy what she knew in her gut about her husband's behavior, she said that she knew his flirting was wrong and that she did not have a problem with undue jealousy. "But then I start to doubt myself and I back down." She knew in her gut that his behavior was inappropriate, but she listened to him and let his words override her own inner voice. Big mistake.

Tammy learned how to quit backing down when she started to listen more carefully to what she knew to be true. She really didn't have to ask her therapist if she thought it was wrong for her husband to openly flirt with other women in front of her, she told me she *knew* it was wrong. So why did she let her husband talk her out of what she knew? She mistakenly told herself that she'd be better off sitting safely in still waters, not rocking the boat. She lacked confidence in herself to handle the rough waters, so she retreated, feeling miserable…because she *knew.*

When Tammy finally opened up to her family and close girlfriend, she gradually gained confidence in her own inner voices. Her friends and family validated her belief, thoughts, and feelings. Her counselor validated her inner knowledge and encouraged her to take risks and respond differently to her husband (her only hope of getting something different back). The next time the flirting happened, she behaved differently. She told him that it hurt her feelings when this happened, that it embarrassed her and made her angry. She told him that she wanted him to stop this behavior and asked if she could count on it not happening again. He attempted to tell her that she was insecure, but this time she simply repeated that she would like for him to stop that behavior and asked again if she could count on it. After about the fourth go-round, he finally yelled, "well, all right!" She had taken a risk when she changed her behavior and didn't retreat, and she not only survived, but she actually got the desired results.

Behaving Assertively

Over the next few weeks Tammy took more risks and, instead of retreating, she set more boundaries with her husband. When he asked her to account for every minute of her time, she told him that it made her feel like a child, and she asked him to treat her like a responsible adult. When he kept pressing for explanations, she just repeated, "I need for you to treat me like a responsible adult." Finally, after she repeated it many times on many occasions, he gave up asking. She changed her behavior; she quit backing down and answering his silly questions. As a result of changing herself, his behavior no longer worked for him, and he eventually gave it up. If we get nothing from a behavior, we will give it up and find a new behavior, and that's a fact.

Tammy was learning how to be assertive. She discovered that by saying how she felt and what she wanted, she was more real and true to herself. She didn't always get what she asked for, but she was far more likely to get it by knowing how to ask for it assertively. Assertiveness is not simply voicing a complaint. A lot of women think that they have been assertive, because they have complained about their spouses' behaviors. They say how they feel; however, they fail to voice what it is they need from their spouses. We will just be labeled whiners if we say how we feel but don't follow it with a clear request for something. I can't overemphasize how important it is to say in clear terms what you want from the person in lieu of the unwanted behavior. In assertiveness, it is important to keep the focus on yourself: "I feel, I need." If you focus on him (e.g., "You did this or that."), then you are more likely to see increased defensiveness in your partner.

Tammy first had to quit blaming, then focus intentionally on her own behavior, and finally take risks by rocking the boat. Her husband was not happy about this change in her at first. What she wanted wasn't always what he wanted, and besides, he had felt more secure when he felt more control over her. However, he gradually became more secure as he saw that Tammy was not abandoning him just because she stood up for what she knew was right. Knowing how to be assertive is the key to knowing how not to give in and back down. Learning the skills of assertiveness is your ticket to standing up for yourself and getting back to who you truly are. You can know your true feelings and desires very well, but if you don't know how to stand up for what you know or how to ask for your desires, you'll never be your true self.

Creating the Congruent Self

Matching Up

The enhanced self is congruent; the lost self is conflicted. The congruent woman will find that what she believes (what she knows to be true), what she says (what comes out of her mouth), and what she does (how she acts) will all match up. So if she *believes* her faith is important to her, when her husband tells her that she doesn't really need to go to worship service, she *says,* "Yes, I do." She then acts on what she knows and says. When he tells her that she needs to stay home instead of visiting her sister that he doesn't like, she *goes* anyway. Her actions, words, and beliefs all match up. A conflicted woman will listen to someone else instead of her gut. She'll say something that she doesn't really believe, just to agree with you, or she may say what she believes, but *do* what you want her to do. If she does this for years, she will end up a conflicted mess. When this internal conflict exists, the person may start to have some sort of physical reaction to the conflict in the form of headaches, digestive problems, anxiety, or depression.

Many women that come into counseling are in conflict with themselves, but think they are in conflict with someone else. Patricia, a thirty-six-year-old woman, came into my office initially to complain about her husband. If you listened to her words alone, he certainly would appear to be the problem. But as a therapist, I looked deeper and listened for what Patricia *knew.* She *knew* that it wasn't okay for her husband to go out drinking every night while she managed the house and the kids alone. She *knew* that her husband had an alcohol problem and she could see that it was destroying her family. She *knew* that it wasn't in her or her children's best interest for him to play golf on Saturday and Sunday and spend no time with the kids. He does sound like the problem, you may say, but since Patricia must be congruent to be at peace, and since she and she alone is responsible for her happiness, then her unhappiness is her problem. What she *knew* was not consistent with how she *acted*. She was behaving in ways that allowed something to continue when it was not consistent with what she *knew* was good for her and the children.

When Patricia got her behavior lined up with what she knew, things improved. She took risks and drew a line in the sand with her husband by firmly stating, "If you want to stay in this marriage you will have to join AA, spend one weekend day with the family, and come home from work in the evening instead of drinking with the boys." He shocked her by meeting her demands; he knew she meant business this time. Had he been unable or unwilling to change, she would have been forced to make a break and pursue her happiness without him. I don't believe that we are supposed to sacrifice our children's happiness or our own for someone who refuses to live responsibly. We are only responsible for changing ourselves, not enabling others' undesirable behavior.

"But He Said..."

I see a lot of women with depression or anxiety symptoms brought on, or exacerbated by, internal conflict. They are often referred to me by a physician because of sleeping and/or eating problems or poor concentration. They sometimes act really confused about the source of the problem or whether there really is a problem. They initially want to believe the problem is solely physiological in nature, in spite of medical evidence to the contrary. I usually begin a woman's therapy by taking a brief history and inquiring about her present circumstances. Little by little she begins to reveal how she really feels and what she really needs.

I'm often astounded when after telling me for nearly an hour about what she knows, she'll then end the session by saying, "I'm so confused, I just don't know; what do you think? Can she really not "know" what she believes about something if I, who have never seen her before, know what she believes after one hour with her? I know only because *she* knows and she has convinced me. She thought she didn't know because somebody else has been telling her something else, and she allowed it to drown out her own inner voice.

Lorie recently came into my office with terrible anxiety and depression. In taking her history, she revealed that she thought her husband might not be faithful to her. As I asked more pointed questions, Lorie talked more specifically about his behavior that led her to be suspicious. She ended by saying, "But I don't really know for sure, so I worry and I feel like I'm going crazy." I looked at her in amazement. She clearly convinced me in just fifty short minutes that her husband is cheating on her. She definitely *knew*, but she didn't listen to herself. Remember: no matter what someone else tells you, your gut feelings should get priority, and *you* deserve to be listened to first.

The congruent person is the person who is true to self and what the self knows in the most private places of the heart. The person who is true to self in her thoughts, words, and actions knows and preserves the true self. The woman that knows herself can then find her passions, the things that make her really happy. She is more content in her relationships because she has less resentment toward others; she hasn't given away what she will later resent. If she's not giving up and giving in just because "he said," then more of her needs are being met. We often blame and resent others if our needs aren't met, when all along we ourselves made the choice to give in or change our course of action just to keep from rocking the boat.

Take a Little Medicine - Forgiveness and Acceptance

Forgiving Yourself

The medicine I'm talking about is not found in a pill; I'm talking about swallowing hard and forgiving not just others, but yourself. Anger at yourself can be just as big a hindrance to your healing as your anger at others. If you take responsibility for what you did to *allow* your partner's bad behavior toward you to continue, then you're less likely to get hung up in anger toward him. Most often you'll find that your partner's behavior wasn't even about you; it was about him being him, doing what he does to get his needs met. The *selfless* woman, however, is just as likely to get angry at herself as she is at others around her. She may turn her anger inward and get depressed as she comes to grips with her years of bad choices, giving up and giving in, and backing down behaviors. She may get so mad at herself that she feels overwhelmed and hopeless about her ability to control her own life.

Friends and family can be a huge help in her desire for change and her need to forgive herself. She needs to seek out a cheering section. If she doesn't have a cheering section among friends or family, she will likely need to seek professional help; that's taking responsibility for fixing herself, no matter what it takes. She will hopefully believe that she is worth the time and the money that a couple of months of therapy will cost her.

Forgiving Others

If you have been looking to someone else to make you happy and blaming them for your current disappointment, then you will not only have to forgive yourself, but you will need to work on forgiving them for their screw ups. However, forgiving someone is not the same as saying that what they did (or are doing) is okay. Not getting hung up in blame and anger toward someone else allows you to move forward to improve yourself and seek your own happiness. Some of you may find forgiveness to be the hardest part of the process. If you are at midlife looking back, you may be looking back at some twenty to thirty years of someone's behavior that *made* you give up valuable parts of yourself. Even if you have had a crisis that led you to take responsibility and focus on your own behavior, you may still harbor anger at your partner.

The most helpful thing you can do to let go of past anger is to stop stacking new anger on top of the old. This allows the old anger to fade further and further into the past. If I stop backing down when you challenge what I know is right for me, then at least I will have less anger toward myself. If I can then view your behavior (assuming it's not harmful to me when I respond in a new self-caring way) as being truly about you, not me, then I can also be less angry at myself. This isn't to say, for example, that someone's insecurity, which leads to controlling behavior, wouldn't still frustrate the heck out of me. Even if I learn to respond by not giving up and giving in when he behaves that way, his behavior will still annoy me.

But being frustrated with a person who is not moving forward in his or her personal growth is different from directly blaming someone for your personal unhappiness. You are sorry that he is lacking in confidence and therefore tries to control you, but you are less angry about it when you don't allow it to change your own behavior and, therefore, who you are. You are accepting that you and your partner are flawed, and you are taking responsibility for not changing your true self in response to one of his flaws. (We'll talk more in Chapter 8 about finding the perfect life without having the perfect partner.) Just remember that the "perfect self" is simply a congruent one.

If a bad behavior continues after you change your response to it, then you have to decide if that behavior will continue to hurt you, even if you no longer give in to it. For example, I don't have to leave my husband if he keeps rolling his eyes when I practice my yoga; I just don't respond to the eye rolling. However, if my husband was making fun of me, calling me old and fat, and didn't stop when I asserted my feelings and needs, I'd have to take more drastic action. We'll discuss enforcement of boundaries with a spouse in more detail in Chapter 9.

Forgiveness doesn't mean that what the other person did doesn't matter to you; it's saying that in spite of the bad way you acted, I forgive you. Staying angry at someone else keeps the focus on that person. In other words, you can't grow yourself if you're focused on someone else. And if you believe forgiveness is "right," then you must behave in a way that matches what you *know.* Holding on to anger hurts the one with the anger and holds that person back from growing and becoming congruent.

"I Can't Change Everything"...Accepting Things I Can't Change

You've come to recognize there are many things that you can change, but you also realize that some things just aren't going to change. You can not make someone else secure or mature, and you may just have to accept him with that flaw...at this time. Changes in your behavior may change the way someone's insecurity *affects* you, but it may not change that person's insecurity. It is in your best interest to accept that you cannot change that person into a secure person. You know that you can't change him; you accept that only he can fix himself if he chooses to. If you don't let another person's flaws change who you are, then you can more easily accept their flaws.

When I was younger I let myself be changed (by giving up and giving in behaviors) by my spouse's flaws and therefore I resented the flaws a lot more. When I took responsibility for my own happiness (waking up from the fairy tale), I changed how I reacted to those flaws and then I found them a lot easier to accept. The real reason that most women are resentful toward their spouses is because they have allowed themselves to be influenced and changed by what they now recognize as flaws in those persons. They may have allowed their partners' insecurity, dishonesty, immaturity, greed, unfaithfulness, or jealousy to influence their own choices in behavior. And these poor choices in behavior lead them to become someone other than who they started out to be.

Some flaws in your partner may lead to behavior that is too dangerous to your body or spirit, and part of being true to your self may include leaving that relationship. These dangerous behaviors are "show stoppers" like physical abuse, addictions, continued infidelity, or relentless psychological and mental abuse. In Chapter 9 we'll talk about setting boundaries when these "show-stopping" behaviors exist and what to do if those boundaries are not respected.

It is usually in your best interest to accept what you can't change, to forgive what has already occurred, and to change the things about yourself that clearly aren't working for you. Although I do believe that there are a few evil people out there, most of us have family or partners who aren't evil or malicious people. Most, like us, behave as they do because they are just trying to get their needs attended to. (Granted, they may have never learned healthy strategies for dealing with satisfying desires.)We can teach them, by our reactions, how to treat us. Every time we let bad behavior work for them we're saying, "This is a good thing; keep it up." Your partner's flawed behavior can do you harm if you change yourself to accommodate his faults. In other words, it's not his shortcomings that hurt you; it's your response to them.

QUESTIONS AND SUGGESTIONS

Question: Can you name one thing that you have changed about yourself in order to keep someone else happy?
Suggestion: Write down the ways in which that person behaved that made you think that you had to "give up and give in." (He rolled his eyes, gave me the silent treatment, or threw a mini-tantrum, for example.)What did you do, or not do, that taught that person that his behaviors will work, and that it's okay for him to treat you that way? For instance, if your partner calls you inappropriate names, what are two things that you do (or don't do) that have enabled it to continue?

Question: Whose voice are you most likely to recognize or listen to, his or yours?
Suggestion: If you answered "his," then next time you feel conflicted or angry because he is telling you something that doesn't match what you know, stop and excuse yourself for a bathroom break. Sit quietly for a few minutes and ask yourself what you know, believe, or feel about this particular thing. Now go out and tell him that you hear what he is saying, but you know or believe ______, and you choose to stick with what you know is right for you. If after a few minutes you still can't hear your inner voice, and still feel confused, tell your partner that you will neither agree nor disagree, but reserve the right to think about it for a while and that you promise to get back to him.

Question: Are you so angry at yourself for years of "giving up and giving in" that you have become depressed and hopeless about change?
Suggestion: Pretend that you are talking to a friend who is in your same predicament. How would you comfort her and advise her as to just one step she might take to get "unstuck"? For instance, you might advise her to do something nice for herself, like getting away for a weekend of solitude in the mountains, or making a weekend visit to her old friend from high school with whom she can reminisce about her "old self." You might invite her to attend an inspiring conference. You might have to advise her to get professional help or assistance.

5 What Women are Longing For (and it Hasn't Got Anything to Do with Sex)

There is a new epidemic out there for which there is no vaccine and little research being done. It's called "loneliness," and it's not only relevant for the little old lady down the street, but also for the young mother and the busy woman in her thirties who find themselves more isolated in today's society. They lack friends who they know well enough to be of any comfort or to share their female experiences. We've all heard it before; you can be in a room with hundreds of people and still be lonely. You can also live in a thriving city, work at a busy job, have a big family, and still be lonely. So goes the state of today's modern woman.

The natural transitions of life, such as choosing a job in another location and marrying and moving away, contribute to our loss of friends, or at least, spending less time with them. In my professional practice, as well as in my life, I have observed a correlation between the holding on of self and the holding on of friends. Those women who have maintained friends over the long haul are more likely to hold on to their true selves over time. Women like me, who at marriage moved far away from friends, family, and all that was familiar, are most vulnerable for giving up pieces of the self. I was particularly vulnerable because I had already moved twice during college and I had not done a good job of keeping in touch with friends. What is the real problem? Did we lose ourselves because we let our friends go, or did we let our selves go and therefore gradually let our friends go? Regardless of why it happened, the solution is the same: find some good women friends.

Women who are making an intentional search for their true selves might first need to get back in touch with the girls they used to be. They can't start their search with just the knowledge of who they are now, since over the years they have changed themselves in ways that have made them unhappy. When we were girls, we hadn't yet been so contaminated with the thoughts, beliefs, and desires of others. Most of us spent the majority of our fun time with other girls—playing, laughing, crying and acting just how we felt. We shared our secrets, our anger, our dreams, and our fears with each other. Those truths about our selves were reflected back to us by our girlfriends. If feedback from our girlfriends helped us figure out who we were in the first place, then it's our girlfriends that can help us rediscover our selves in adulthood.

Developmental Changes Contributing to Our Loss of Girlfriends In Our Twenties

We enjoyed such closeness with our girlfriends, but then boys got our attention. By the time we reached our twenties we were seriously locked into the fairy tale and the search for Mister Right. In our early twenties we preferred a group of good-looking men over a group of fun women any day. We allowed the hunt for Mister Right to consume all of our time and energy, until at last our dream boy was located.

He was so cute that we forgot about everything else except being together and doing the things that made him happy. We lost touch with a few friends here and there, but after all, he was the one that we really wanted. We gradually gave up all other activities, devoting all of our free time to the prince and losing sight of the importance of other women in our lives.

I was as guilty as most in this area, focusing on the "love of my life" and letting friendships suffer from lack of time and attention. Instead of spending time with a friend, I chose to sit and wait, hoping *he* would call. This is one of those areas where women are still making the same mistakes. Teenage girls in high school, females in college, and women in early adulthood twenties are guilty of allowing men to totally dominate their time and energies. As a result, they cut themselves off from the support, encouragement, and validation they would get from women friends.

I am seeing Beth, a twenty-four-year-old woman who complains of anxiety and mild depression. Beth moved to our area, leaving her family behind, and so lacks friends with whom to socialize. It wasn't until our third session that she revealed that she had a relationship with a guy named Todd living two and a half hours away and she had been dating him for seven years. He makes excuses about why he can't come to visit her on the weekends, and she almost always is the one to rearrange her schedule to go and visit him. After seven years he still can't make up his mind about marrying her and tells her that it is because she lacks confidence and needs to work on herself first.

The problem is that Beth has no women friends; she invests all of her free time in Todd who criticizes her constantly, and this of course does not contribute to her confidence. I am encouraging her to spend more time pursuing women friends and less time pursuing Todd. Girlfriends will help her "get real" and give her more honest feedback about herself and what's going on in her life and relationships. I told her to plan something with friends and tell Todd that she is too busy to drive to his place. If he really cares about her, he will be concerned enough to get in the car and drive the two and one half hours to inquire about the change he has observed. I suspect that if she had a few close women friends, she wouldn't need a therapist to validate her beliefs.

Some women in their twenties and thirties are spending most of their time in pursuit of Mister Right, and if they marry at this point, they are then preoccupied with their new husbands, their new homes and new lives. If they aren't careful, they might just forget how important their women friends are. With less feedback from friends of the same sex, they may fail to recognize the little changes that are starting to erode their true selves.

In Our Thirties

By the time many women are in their thirties they are focused on children and their well-being. We chase small children, take them to dance and sports activities, and faithfully attend parent-teacher conferences. Even when we dare take time for ourselves by spending it with friends, it tends to be child-focused or couple-focused. I remember longing for the company and companionship of other women during those years when I was staying home with small children. But I felt that I should take care of my social needs during my husband's work day, so as not to interfere with "his" time. I occasionally invited other mothers and their little ones over for coffee or lunch, but it usually turned into near chaos. Women with children know what a challenge it is to have an intelligent conversation when babies are causing continuous interruptions. Doing things with other women and their children had its purpose, but I needed time with friends away from children as well.

In Our Forties

In our forties many women are unbelievably productive, caught up in so many activities that we barely have time to think. Some forty-something women have been promoted to increased responsibilities at work just as the kids are approaching their teens and their spiraling activities. The pace picks up dramatically and unexpectedly; we mistakenly thought we would have more time for ourselves when our children were a bit older and could do more. Instead, we find that new demands have replaced the old, and we are now attending sports events or driving adolescents to social events.

In addition to increased activity at home, many women now have jobs with greater responsibilities. Guilt about not being available to kids because of work causes women to compensate by spending all of their free time with family. The validation and companionship that they get from friends is sacrificed. Because men grew up expecting to spend most of their days at work, they have less guilt about not being with the kids. Men are also less likely to feel guilty about taking time away from the kids when asked to play four hours of golf on Saturday. A woman is more likely to say no if asked to participate in a four-hour activity on her day off.

Before we know it, it is time to pick out curtains for the dorm room and help the kids pack for college. In addition to all of this frantic external activity, women in their forties are approaching an internal crisis of "meaning." As they enter midlife, they may be singing that old song, "Is That All There Is?" The external chaos turns to internal chaos and she may start to question every choice she's made in her life. Maybe she realizes her losses (self and friends), maybe she will have a "midlife crisis," and maybe she will begin her search for rediscovery of self. This is a great time for friends if she has them, but there's not a lot of energy left for making them if she doesn't.

In Our Fifties

If you were one of those smart women who maintained friendships with other women in spite of your busy life, then by fifty you should be enjoying the comfort of close girlfriends. Far too many women, however, find themselves isolated by the time they are approaching midlife; they feel disappointed and disillusioned about life in general and have no one in their lives that seems to understand. They have been so preoccupied with the business of life, jobs, and family that they have neglected to treat themselves to the joys of friendship and fun. They may have failed to even notice the loneliness that was quietly, and very gradually, setting in.

For the majority of modern women taking care of their homes and families was mostly their responsibilities, but by fifty women usually have less to "run." She's tired of tending to the house, the dust, the laundry, and the kitchen. Maybe the nicest thing she could do for herself during this life transition is to spend time with other women. Friends will share their thoughts and validate her experience, and, before she knows it, there'll be moments when she's acting like her old self again. Many women at midlife are figuring out that they are empowered when they are able to be themselves, and they are celebrating this newfound joy with their girlfriends. And be aware: Men are often frightened by this show of power; so if women look to men alone for friendship during their transition, they might be subtly discouraged.

You may argue that these are natural stages of life and the changes they bring can't really be avoided. It's true that these developments are quite normal, but I believe it is all about attitudes and *choices*. It must be an *intentional* choice to find and maintain friendships. It is my hope that young women will figure out early on that they can *choose* to intentionally make girlfriends a priority in their lives.

Societal Changes Contributing to the Isolation of Women

Loss of Natural Support Groups

The signs of loneliness seem to be showing themselves at earlier and earlier stages of life, and there are a couple of reasons for this. A century ago women had a natural support system; most often married someone from the community in which they grew up. Girlfriends from childhood, teachers who taught them as children, cousins, aunts and uncles, and their siblings were all living right around them. When these women had a problem, they had a river of experience to call upon, lots of validation, and plenty of offers to help. Women are empowered when they are validated by support groups.

These natural support groups of years ago no longer exist for the majority of women in this country. With every decade that passes, families seem to spread farther and farther apart. You grow up in Georgia, go to college in Michigan, marry a guy from Chicago, and move to Seattle for his new job. The prohibitive costs of plane tickets and long-distance phone calls kept the relationships that were once so important more and more distant; you functioned more and more as an island and you were more isolated from the people who knew your original self.

My husband and I lived in Washington, DC, after we were married. His family was five hours away in Connecticut and mine was nine hours away in South Carolina. In the big city it was easy to find other young people who, like us, were miles away from their families, and who, like us, were looking for friends. We were both fortunate to make new friends who were there for us in the absence of our "natural support systems." These new friends, however, didn't know the old me, the original me before the fairy tale took hold, and therefore never challenged any new behaviors or new ways of thinking that appeared. After all, everything is new to a new friend; how could they distinguish between the real self and the new, changed self? Again, changes in the original self aren't necessarily all bad—just the ones made in response to a false belief.

The Rat Race

Another reason for loneliness arriving at earlier stages of life is that we are living in a society that seems to move at a much faster pace.

Perpetual motion and a hidden message that we should be productive every moment keep us from having time to invest in developing our network of support. It keeps us from playfulness, too, which can be far more renewing than a day at the gym. Friendships take time, something we all seem to be lacking. And when we sacrifice friendships, we're also sacrificing a big piece of ourselves, our support, our fun, and our healing laughter. Young women in their thirties who have small kids and work outside the home are so frazzled they don't even realize that loneliness is a big part of their sadness or mood swings.

It's easy to get caught up in this rat race and fall victim to it. If your neighbor has her boys in three sports, you wonder if yours are going to miss out if you don't follow suit. I heard one mother say, "If they don't start soccer when they're four, then how will they compete and be good enough to make the team in high school?" So now she feels the pressure to put her kid in at least three sports, because how does she know which ones he'll like when he's fourteen? Kids today are so scheduled that they actually have little time to just play. As a result, they won't have to wait until they are older to lose the art of play, because they will never fully learn the art of free, unstructured play as children.

I remember feeling frazzled leaving the office and running into a crowded grocery store because it was my turn to buy the team's sport drinks (water is apparently no longer acceptable). Now if a child has two soccer games and two baseball games a week, then his mother has her work cut out for her. And since he must be well rounded, you are compelled to have him in piano or drama classes as well. It sounds ridiculous, but young mothers get caught up in trying to prove that they're as competent as the mothers next door and that their kids can do just as well as other neighbor's. Common sense is forgotten, and what's worse is that they are genuinely convinced by our driven society that their kids really need to be doing all these activities.

Our level of chaos is also greatly enhanced by cell phones and much of the other new technology that is supposed to save us time. I feel obligated to talk more on the phone when I have 7000 minutes of night and weekend time, and with a world of knowledge at my fingertips, how can I not get on the computer everyday? Email can be another time robber; I'm as guilty as the next in wasting time with junk mail, not true personal communication. These communication devices can be used to enhance relationships or they can be used as a substitute for real relationships. Unfortunately, I see people becoming more disconnected in spite of the increased number of hi-tech devices available to keep them "connected."

Too many women are spending time in online chat rooms, only serving to move them further away from meaningful relationships with real people. And why are people chatting with perfect strangers that they can't touch or see anyway? They are lonely, but reaching in the wrong direction. I see families who are breaking up because someone in the marriage has become addicted to the internet and has neglected not only friendships but spouses and children.

Too much time on cell phones or the internet can add to the hectic pace for today's modern woman. Whether it's her husband's overuse of the internet or her own, it will rob her of much needed time to connect in a real way with women friends. Being "connected to the world" sounds better than it is and can seduce us into a false sense of connectedness. My time with girlfriends is time *away* from the rat race of life.

Loss of Control = Loss of Friends

I am referring here to the control we must have over ourselves and our own choices. When I give up my control to someone else, I am then choosing to do what someone else wants by meeting their needs, not my own. Some women I see become isolated because their husbands or boyfriends demand all of their free time. During the romantic stage of the relationship, they were flattered by this constant demand for attention, but too often, it becomes a manipulation and a way to maintain control and power over a woman. Sometimes the control is quite subtle and sometimes it's blatant. Susan, a client, told me that every time she tried to plan to get together with a girlfriend, her husband would wait until the last minute and then come up with a conflict that would prevent him from watching the kids. It would then be too late for her to find a sitter. She also discovered that he did not give her phone messages from friends. A few years later, when Susan was going through a nasty divorce, this woman lacked the validation, comfort, and support that girlfriends can offer. She was able to reflect back and talk about the control her husband had over her in earlier times, admitting that she recognized it, but failed to do anything about it.

Some women tell me that their husbands say they should spend all of their free time with them, and act hurt if they choose to be with girlfriends. Women who have a fear of conflict, and therefore try to please everybody, will cave in to this kind of manipulation. They may also feel responsible for his happiness and then experience guilt—inappropriate guilt—because he's not happy. But remember, we teach people how to treat us, and this woman taught her husband that if he pouts or yells loud enough, she will give up something she really needs.

What Happens When Women Are Isolated? Lack of Validation for Being Ourselves

I want to add a few thoughts about the effects of isolation and a lack of validation by those we trust. The vast majority of women that I see are lacking in confidence, and most of those lacking in confidence are sorely lacking in friends. Those that have no family nearby are the women who seem to be the least secure and most vulnerable. When we are lacking a base of support, we may be weaker and less able to stand up for what we know, less likely to ask for what we need, and less able to enforce our boundaries.

Lack of Validation for the Tough Job of Parenting

One of the worst effects isolation has on many women is the lack of feedback and validation regarding the difficult job of parenting. When my oldest son was being very difficult and hard to manage, I was starting to doubt myself and my own parenting skills. I was fairly new in the town to which we'd moved and not well connected with friends at that time. I heard little about the problems of other kids. Fortunately, I had great neighbors across the street: a Lutheran minister, his wife, and their two children (one of which was the same age as my son). Martha was chatting with me in the yard one day about some outrageous thing her son had done and how she had handled it. We were able to share our "isn't it awful" feelings and laugh at the kids' misdeeds. I felt so relieved to find that I wasn't the only one experiencing difficult behavior; she also validated my approach to solving the problem. Isolated young mothers, without other young mothers to share their concerns, frustrations, and doubts, might begin to experience inappropriate guilt and shame about their children's failures or problem behaviors. They are also more likely to doubt their own response to that child's troubling behavior.

Our youngest child is now a teenager and if I didn't talk regularly with friends who are raising teens, I'd be miserable. Sometimes when I listen to their stories about their children's misbehavior I feel better; sometimes I feel the opposite. Either way, it gives me a yardstick against which to measure what I'm doing or not doing. It helps me check myself. Of course, it doesn't mean that I always change what I'm doing if my friend is doing something else. But if four of my friends think I'm being too tough on my child, then I might want to take a second look and at least re-evaluate what I'm doing.

During childrearing years we also need to occasionally get away from our kids and our spouses. An evening out with other women is renewing; that wonderful camaraderie not only validates our daily experience, but it reminds us that we are more than moms and wives.

Women in midlife will tell you not to wait until the kids are leaving for college to have a night out. We need our friends to rescue us from the doldrums of routine housework and the daily demands of children.

This can pose a challenge for young mothers with husbands who have convinced their wives they aren't capable of watching the kids. Years later these women will wish they would have patted their spouses on the back, assured them that all would survive, and gone on to share in the fun and support of their women friends. Those who gave up time with friends because they feared their husband would let the kids get into trouble often realize they made unnecessary sacrifices.

Lack of Validation for Partnering

Another important thing that friends do for us, especially in the early stages of dating and marriage, is to give us feedback about our thoughts, feelings, and behavior in our relationships with our partners. Women who come into therapy for relationship counseling sometimes do so because they lack girlfriends to validate their experience. When a woman knows in her gut that she is being controlled, put down, manipulated, or deceived, it is often through the validation of friends that she gets the courage to act on it.

This isn't to say that if you have friends you will never need counseling for relationship problems. Some problems are so complicated that they are outside the scope of our friend's expertise, and that is when professional help may be required. Women tend to let relationship problems slide until their mood is seriously affected, the problem is huge, or a crisis has arisen. If the problem becomes overwhelming, professional crisis intervention might be necessary.

Sue, a thirty-eight-year-old woman, came to me after getting involved with a man who she saw as her true soul mate. She was head over heels in love, and in her blind romantic state, she failed to see a few brightly colored flags that her friends couldn't help but notice. He often "forgot" his wallet when they went out to eat. He started talking about moving in and doing some work on her house a short time after they started dating. He would lose his temper and say degrading things to her, but then be apologetic and bring her flowers. Sue later found out that he was visiting an old girlfriend when he said he was visiting his parents. But he was sorry, and she was so in love. Her girlfriends told her what they saw, invalidating the fairy tale view that she held onto so tightly. She kept making excuses for him, but finally her girlfriends convinced her to see a counselor. When the counselor was unable to validate her fairy tale version of reality, she started to get real—first with herself, then with her boyfriend. I have no doubt she would have stayed in this bad relationship had it not been for the intervention of girlfriends.

Sometimes women wake up in midlife and realize they no longer *like* the individuals to whom they are married. They may *love* the people with whom they've shared a life with for twenty years, but now that they have transformed themselves, they no longer particularly *like* them. Many women choose to stay with their long-time partner. These women may have to get more of their companionship needs met through their girlfriends. They may no longer have fun with their partners, and all efforts to inspire them to turn off the television have failed. They are depressed because they are lonely; their husbands are not able to meet their need for companionship or friendship.

Beth, one such client, had never been anywhere outside of North Carolina because her husband didn't want to travel. When I finally convinced her to take responsibility for her own happiness, she began to take trips with women friends. Now she can't be held down; she's a cruising maniac! It's much healthier for women at this age to get more involved with girlfriends than to have affairs or get overly involved in their grown children's lives. Such friends can understand your desire to keep your marriage together, as well as your right to meet your needs in other healthy ways. Girlfriends play important roles in helping us be real and true to ourselves in relationships, as well as helping us resolve some needs for fun and sharing.

OUR SPECIAL NEED FOR GIRLFRIENDS IN MIDLIFE

Getting Through Menopause

There's a lot going on in midlife, and if we ever needed friends, it's now. The demands of life with children are changing, our bodies are changing, and our relationships with spouses are changing. The physical changes are disconcerting, and men can't help us because they are even more baffled than we are. Changes like loss of libido, memory loss, physical appearance, and energy level. There is a lot of confusion about menopause and what women can and cannot safely do to combat its symptoms and effects. Fortunately, women of this age are more open, and it is the sharing of new information and personal experiences that keeps them sane during this menopausal upheaval.

My husband and I were invited to dinner at a friend's house a few months ago and, as usual, the men congregated downstairs and the women sat upstairs and chatted. Two of the women I had never met before, but within a very short time we were all sharing our very personal menopausal experiences and knowledge. Within minutes, these women knew about my sex drive, my choice not to take hormones, and how many hot flashes I had! We discussed alternatives to traditional medical treatment, and when we left, each of us knew something that we didn't know before. Women have a remarkable ability to "connect on short notice," allowing for a deeper level of relating right from the beginning. I later asked my husband what the men were talking about and he said they were discussing business, the market, and, of course, sports.

Last night I went to a concert and saw a middle-aged woman squeeze down the row in front of me and sit beside another middle-aged woman. The woman getting seated introduced herself, and before long the two were deep in conversation. I only heard bits and pieces of the conversation, but their talk concerned frustrations about menopause, dry skin, and what medications work. I just love the way women will connect and share personal information like that, and I had to laugh when I tried to picture two men talking about their spreading waistlines or thinning hair, and what they might try for it.

Networking…It's A Woman Thing

By their middle years many women are masters at "networking." Historically, women haven't been the ones in charge, so this skill was probably learned out of necessity. Women had to learn more roundabout ways of getting information or things they needed—usually through other women—who would then direct them to the person in charge. This networking isn't just about getting a service; it's a key way women connect as they help each other succeed. In Gail Sheehey's book, "*New Passages,*" she quotes Elizabeth Stevenson, the Jungian analyst, as saying, "Men may be very powerful in the world, but emotionally they're pretty starved. And we have a lot of life in us. I mean, look at this decade! The 'networking' among women is a connective tissue that is very much part of the feminine principle, and we are loaded with it, just loaded with it. Men mostly are very scared of it. So women and men find themselves pretty far apart at this point, with the potential for a lot of envy."

New Needs, New Values

I think we can all agree that the middle years are a time of drastic change, and we know that change creates stress. When women are under stress, they need validation and support. For those who didn't isolate themselves during childrearing years, they now have a strong network of girlfriends to lend a listening ear, women going through the same changes or those who are a couple of years ahead of them that can now offer sound, practical advice.

When a woman hits the midlife marker, she is less likely to be facing life with a romanticized outlook. She is now faced with the cold reality that her life is certainly half over, and she now values life in a new way. Most of us are more appreciative of life in general now; we try to live more in the moment, not taking anything for granted as we may have in our younger years. One of the things that we may have taken for granted is friendship, or the value of women friends.

As women age they aren't as competitive as they were when they were younger, and therefore can more easily value and embrace each other. Younger women often view each other as a threat and tend to compete not only for male attention, but for friends. One young woman complains that one girlfriend is jealous if she spends time with other girlfriends. One young woman is jealous of her friend because of the way she flirts with her husband. Most women over fifty don't want your husband; they're saying, "One is quite enough, thank you very much."

Younger women are more likely to compete through their children, too, taking a "mine is a better student than yours," or "mine is a better soccer player than yours" position. Women approaching their middle years can talk more openly about their problems with children and how their kids are worrying them; they really don't need so much to impress you with their children's accomplishments.

Need For Empowerment

Women who lack friends generally lack power. The best example of friendship's empowering effects on women is played out in the old movie, *Fried Green Tomatoes*. Kathy Bate's character is transformed as the movie progresses. She is initially almost invisible to her husband, as well as others. She makes efforts to revive her stale marriage by cooking romantic dinners and acting sexy, only to have her insensitive husband grab his plate off the table and sit in front of the TV. She feels useless, powerless, and walked on by others. She hides candy bars and comforts herself by overeating. It is in her friendship with Mrs. Threadgood where she finds strength and gets on a different path. My favorite scene is when Bates is trying desperately to find a parking spot at a crowded grocery store. Two young, cocky girls whip into a space that she is trying to get, yelling to her, "We're younger and faster." You can see the transformation taking place in her eyes. She begins to ram the young girl's Volkswagen repeatedly. She screams out, "TWANDA," a name symbolizing the strength and power she now feels. When the young women come running out of the store and ask her what she thinks she's doing, she says, "I'm older and I have more insurance." From that moment on she acted like someone who had control over her own life – she felt and acted empowered.

Friends Relieve Stress—A Study You Won't Believe!

There is some fascinating research about how differently women react to stress than men. An article by Gale Berkowitz about a UCLA study on how women cope with stress states: "Scientists now suspect that hanging out with our friends can actually counteract the kind of stomach-quivering stress most of us experience on a daily basis. A landmark UCLA study suggests that women respond to stress with a cascade of brain chemicals that cause us to make and maintain friendships with other women. It's a stunning find that has turned five decades of stress research—most of it on men—upside down." It goes on to say, and I summarize, that instead of women only secreting hormones that make us want to fight or flee, women have a larger behavioral repertoire as they release the hormone, oxytocin, which buffers the old "fight or flight" response and encourages her to tend children and gather with other women instead.

Dr. Laura Cousin Klein, Ph. D. , Assistant Professor of Biobehavioral Health at Penn State University, says that when women engage in this "tending or befriending," more oxytocin is released which further counters stress and produces a calming effect. "This calming response does not occur in men," says Dr. Klein, "because testosterone—which men produce in high levels when they're under stress—seem to reduce the effects of oxytocin. Estrogen," she adds, "seems to enhance it." Gale Berkowitz, the article's author, adds that friendships "soothe our tumultuous inner world, fill the emotional gaps in our marriage, and help us remember who we really are."

Who would have guessed that this drive and need for friends that I have experienced, and seen other women among my clients experience, would be hormonal? I've just given several circumstantial reasons why it's in our best interest to pursue friends in adulthood, and here is a biological one. As I said earlier, many women fail to recognize their lack of friendships as one possible cause for the sadness, agitation, or anxiety with which they struggle daily.

HOW DO I MAKE FRIENDS? I've Never Been Good At It

I won't tell you how much you need friends without offering a few tips on how to make it happen. Many women, lacking in self confidence, feel uncertain about where to begin in searching for and making friends. Perhaps they are introverts and fear that they are too quiet to be interesting, or won't know how to keep a conversation going. Maybe they are just so caught up in the "rat race" that they believe they can't make time for friends. Some women are simply not going to the right places to meet other women. They have gotten themselves into such a rut so that their only outings are to the discount store or the grocery store! So even though you are acknowledging your need for friends, you might be asking the question, "How can I make friends when I don't really know where to go?"

Get Real and Use Rational Self-Talk

You have to be willing to step out and go somewhere. Let me remind you of the fact that, unlike when you were six years old, people don't come knocking on your door asking you to come out and play. (I miss that, don't you?) But you are more prepared to face reality at this age, so get real; the doorbell isn't going to ring. You have to take responsibility for *your* need and *do* something to meet that need. If there are not a lot of potential friends in your neighborhood or at your workplace, then you will have to put yourself in other places. When I first moved to Nebraska, where I knew no one, I joined a jazzercise class. I left my kids in the nursery, which gave me time to chat with other women before and after class. Later, we started going out to lunch after the class. Within weeks, we started getting together outside of class just to socialize. When I moved to North Carolina, I joined a beginner's tennis class and a club called Newcomers. People won't come find you just because you are new in town; but you will have to go find them.

You also have to get over your fear of rejection and reason with yourself about the following things: (1) If someone says "no" when I ask them to do something, it doesn't necessarily mean they don't like me; it could just mean they are genuinely unavailable at that particular time. Remember the crazy pace at which we're all treading. You have the sense to know if someone is telling you they flat don't want to spend time with you. If someone says they are busy on that date, but would really love to go, I might say, "Well, what day would work for you? I'm dying to see that movie." Now if I've done all of that and they still say they can't find a time that will work, then I still don't totally give up. I respect their boundaries and put the ball back in their court in this way: "Well, I'd love to get together sometime, so give me a call if your schedule frees up." If they don't return the call, then accept this isn't a potential friend for now. *Don't make it about you*. It's about that person and whatever is going on with them at that time. (2) Tell yourself, "I don't like everybody and not everybody will like me—and that's OK." If we go around with the irrational belief that everybody *should* like us, then we set ourselves up for certain disappointment. But if I accept that everyone doesn't have to like me, then I'm more likely to calmly receive that message. And again, it doesn't mean that there's anything wrong with me. I have my preferences, why shouldn't others have theirs?

"...But I'm an Introvert"

If you are slightly or seriously introverted, you may need to work on your assertiveness skills before you feel able to reach out and ask people for what you want. I also work to convince introverts to *accept* shyness as part of their makeup, and not view it as a flaw. If you see yourself as "flawed" because you're not an extrovert, then you won't have the confidence you desire. Let's face it, extroverts need introverts, otherwise we'd all be talking at the same time and nobody would be listening!

It will undoubtedly be harder for a shy person to reach out and initiate, but so what? You, my friend, are quite capable with difficult tasks. Most of the introverted women that I talk to fear they are being viewed as boring or dull around other women. As an introvert, you simply have to be able to ask open-ended questions. For instance, "Tell me about your job" or "Tell me what brought you here." Most people like talking about themselves, and these conversation starters lead them to do most of the talking. You really don't have to introduce some breathtaking topic; just show genuine interest in others and whatever it is that's important to them.

Be a Friend to Get a Friend

Be real about the fact that if you don't have friends, it's probably because you haven't been a friend. My mother used to complain about people not coming to see her, but I never saw her make any effort to visit or call them. Maybe you're not sure how to be a friend. Let's talk about a few practical "how to's" when it comes to being or making a friend. We all enjoy and need to feel the care and concern of others. You don't have to do big things or be a great conversationalist to make someone else feel important or cared about. Sit down and think about what you wish *you* had from a friend and then *do* some of those things for someone else. Since we behave our way to being what we want to be, you have to behave like a friend to be a friend. Quit waiting for someone else to do it first. Take responsibility for your own happiness. Be intentional.

Go out and buy some greeting cards for different special occasions. You might even buy some of those "for no reason at all" cards and send one to a friend out of the blue. It's such a nice feeling to know someone was thinking of you. And don't underestimate the power of food! You can always take brownies over to a new neighbor, even if she's been living there for six months before you get around to it. (It's never too late to receive cash or chocolate.)

Over the years I've learned to forget about keeping score. When I was younger, I was more likely to stop and figure out who called who last, or who had who over for dinner last. Now if I get the urge to get together with someone, I couldn't care less about whether who called last. If I'm feeling the desire for support or laughter, then it's my responsibility alone to get what I need. I may have to call four or five women before I find someone who is free for lunch. As we get more secure in ourselves, we don't give up so easily; "no" is not a rejection, but a decline on this particular invitation.

Be More Accepting and Forgiving

Last but not least, let's talk about two necessary ingredients of friendship that improve with maturity. My *acceptance* and *forgiveness* have improved with age, and have greatly enhanced my ability to be a friend. It sounds simplistic, but the old Golden Rule really fits here. We must accept the imperfections of our friends as we hope and pray they will accept ours. You must accept that Linda gets enthusiastic and often interrupts before you can get your sentence out. You need to forgive Mandy for not inviting you to her son's wedding. If you're going to have friends that are part of the human race, you'll have to accept imperfections. This can be tricky at times because there is always a fine line that separates an acceptable flaw from one that makes us feel used or abused. As in any relationship, we must take responsibility for keeping toxic stuff out of our lives.

QUESTIONS AND SUGGESTIONS

Question: Can you identify life-stage events or circumstances that have pulled you away from friends or increased your isolation? Can you identify one good girlfriend that you lost touch with over the years?
Suggestion: Try to recall friends that you knew back when. What pulled you apart? If you were able to identify one female friend from your past, attempt to re-establish that friendship by making a phone call or writing a letter. There's nothing wrong with saying, "I'm so mad at myself for letting the crazy pace of life keep us out of contact with each other…"

Question: If you see yourself as isolated, is it possible that you have neglected people who are potential friends?
Suggestion: First, make a list of all the women you currently know but have neglected. Include neighbors, wives of spouse's friends, acquaintances related to work, church or synagogue, or social groups. Circle one that you think has potential for a real friendship. List three ways that you wish that person would reach out to you in friendship. Now do those three things to reach out to that person.

Question: If you are new in your community or just very isolated, are you wondering where to meet new people?
Suggestion: Think in categories. Make columns on a piece of paper with categories such as spiritual, intellectual, sports, physical exercise, arts and crafts, political – and any others you can think of. Now under each category, list any activity that you might enjoy. For instance, under "exercise"

you might write "yoga," or under "art" you might write "watercolor class," or under "political" you might write "volunteer in campaign." Under each activity write at least one place where you might go. For example, you might find yoga at the YMCA, and a watercolor class at the community center. All of the places to which you go are potential opportunities to meet other women with similar and new interests.

6

The Grouping Trend of the New Millennium

There is a definite trend developing among modern women, especially those approaching forty and beyond. Women are finding any excuse under the sun to form groups—and what's more, many of them tout "fun" as their only objective! Although fun may be their stated purpose, these groups are providing much more than what is on the surface. These women, in search of their true selves, can find support, encouragement, and empowerment through grouping with other women.

Women's groups give women the opportunity to support each other, whether it be for intellectual growth, spiritual growth, physical strength, or just for fun. They provide a network of friends to carry us through the inevitable changes brought about by time, but, most importantly, groups provide an opportunity for the celebration of the whole self. Women across America are responding to the isolation they have experienced due to their too-busy lives, or distance from family, by forming a wide variety of groups.

I've never seen or heard of so many excuses for forming women's groups. *Oprah* recently did a show entitled, "Girls Night Out," and groups from all over the country were part of the audience. There were the "Biker Babes," the "Cultured Pearls," the "Charity Girls," and the "Sole Sisters," just to name a few. One group vowed to do something adventurous and out of their comfort zone once a month. One group just met for girl time, but always wore their pearls. The Charity Girls met to help out the needy in their community, and the Sole Sisters were really into funky shoes. My favorite of all girlfriend groups was on *Good Morning America*. These young moms called themselves "Cheaper Than Therapy" and met regularly (without kids) to talk about everyday life stresses, kids, and marriage.

GROUPING JUST FOR FUN

Sweet Potato Queens

Up until last year, I felt guilty for simply lying on the couch to watch a thirty-minute television show. Now I spend more time than I care to confess shopping for the perfect tiara or looking for matching outfits for my own women's group. We are a Sweet Potato Queen chapter—twelve fun-loving, adventurous, spicy women ranging from ages forty five to sixty five. We all have busy lives, but when we get together and hail ourselves as "queens," we allow our fun sides to be celebrated as we share pure joy and laughter.

Jill Conner Browne, author of *The Sweet Potato Queens Book of Love*, tells how she wanted to be a high-school beauty queen but thought she had to have big boobs and big red hair – neither of which she possessed. Many years later she talked her girlfriends into entering the St. Patrick's Day parade as "beauty queens." An uncle had a sweet potato farm so they decided to call themselves "Sweet Potato Queens" and throw sweet potatoes to the crowd. They wore big red wigs and stuffed their boobs, giving them the bust lines any queen would die for. Majorette boots, tacky green sequin dresses and, of course, tiaras finished off the outfits. The crowd loved it, and the parade now boasts hundreds of self-proclaimed beauty queens.

When Ms. Conner Browne wrote her book about her experience with love, men, relationships, and food, it started an international movement of middle-aged women followers…wannabes, she calls them (SPQ wannabes). In her wisdom, she knew that every woman longs to be recognized as the queen that she really is. To prove this, there are currently more than 8,274 registered queens out there, and probably many more that are having too much fun to take time out to register.

In my own defense, I haven't become a self-centered party girl, and I haven't had a midlife breakdown. I still work at my respected profession, I still effectively parent my eighteen-year-old, I still occasionally cook, and I even vacuum when absolutely necessary. But in addition to these roles, I am being my old self again—playing pranks, hanging out with other women, and laughing my head off. This added dimension, being part of a women's group, gives my life that secret ingredient, that spice that you add to the recipe that zips it up and makes it taste unique and special. And it has other advantages as well. One Sweet Potato Queen wannabe in North Carolina told me that when her teenage son acts up, she just threatens to show up at his school wearing her short, green, sequined parade outfit with the wig, tiara, and majorette boots. Now that, my friend, is a genuine threat to a fifteen-year-old.

The Red Hat Society

I recently reread the poem that was the inspiration for the start of the Red Hat Society, and it influenced me greatly. The poem is called *Warning* by Jenny Joseph and it begins by saying, "When I am an old woman…" and goes on to state all the unconventional things she will do when she gets "old"—like wearing purple with a red hat and stockpiling impractical items.

The colors (red and purple) of the Red Hat Society are like a badge of honor for women over fifty, and their hope is to change the negative perception of aging. When you look at their website, one of the first headings you will see is, "Greeting middle age with nerve, humor and élan. It goes on to say, "Silliness is the comedy relief of life, and since we are all in it together, we might as well join red-gloved hands and go for the gusto together. Underneath the frivolity, we share a bond of affection, forged by common life experiences and a genuine enthusiasm for wherever life takes us next."

I recently interviewed several women from the local Red Hat Mamas chapter. Eunice Query is ninety-three-years old, single, and describes herself as a "nonagenarian." This particular group has thirty members but averages about eighteen for each monthly gathering. When I asked, "What do you all do?" she laughed joyfully and said, "Nothing!" They have no officers, no dues, no program, and no fundraisers; they meet just for fun. And it all began when two women sent out thirty invitations. They were disappointed when they didn't get responses but were pleasantly surprised when eighteen women actually showed up. The group has been growing strong ever since.

GROUPING FOR HEALTH AND FITNESS

You may be getting what you need spiritually, intellectually, and having all the fun you can handle, but you recognize that you just aren't in the best physical shape. Whether it's losing weight, working out, or participation in a sport, it'll be easier and a lot more fun in a group. In a same-sex group you'll get encouragement on the days you don't have the motivation you need. My client, Rhonda, is a good example. She felt badly about her weight and wanted to lose thirty pounds, but repeatedly got discouraged halfway through her diet plan. When she grouped up with three other women who were trying to lose weight, she did better. She had people call who would understand when she felt like caving in and giving up the struggle.

Walking groups not only provide exercise, but when women walk together, they talk together. If you are a stay-at-home mom you could set a time to meet in the mornings and push strollers as you walk. You might even reward yourselves with a monthly girls' night out while your husbands watch the kids. Many a relationship crisis or problem has been processed while strolling the neighborhood. As with all women's groups, in an exercise group, we end up getting more out of it than was originally intended.

GROUPS FOR YOUR SPECIAL INTEREST

Some women just aren't going to act silly; it's just not who they are. They don't, however, have to forfeit the benefits of grouping with other women. There are many groups formed around serious topics or topics of special interest. Women can enjoy each other's company while doing or learning more about gardening, crafts, games like chess or scrabble, antiquing, animal rescue or political issues.

Just as fun activities can sprout from a serious-minded group, serious activities can sprout from a group that starts with "fun" as their purpose. Our Vintage Jewel Queens group met to celebrate Deb's birthday and to discuss an upcoming trip. Deb suggested that we begin to support a cause, and we all agreed on the battered women's shelter in our area. Someone else thought it would be fun to dress up in our parade outfits and go to the local nursing home to pamper the women there with manicures. (We imagined ourselves sitting in a nursing home in the future and decided that getting our nails painted would brighten *our* day.) Our group started because we needed more fun in our lives, but now that we are having so much fun, we are looking for ways to reach out and share that with others.

GROUPING FOR SPIRITUAL GROWTH AND ENCOURAGEMENT

On Wednesday mornings I drive past a Baptist church where the parking lot is always full. Each time I passed by, I saw only women getting out of the cars, and I wondered what was going on. I called the church and was told that it was a women's Bible study that wasn't really connected to that church. There are currently more women's Bible studies, spiritual growth groups, and prayer groups offered than ever before. Church-affiliated groups, as well as independent, nondenominational groups, are very available to women searching for support in their spiritual journey.

Small Groups and Spiritual Retreats

I hear a lot of women say that they go to worship services but still feel disconnected. They find it virtually impossible to form meaningful relationships in such a large group. Joining a small group within a larger one is the best way to really get to know people. In my large church, I also felt quite disconnected until I took a small group Bible study class that met weekly. Until then, I came and went, just saying a quick "hello" to those passing by. Even my Sunday school class was large, and although I got a lot from the lesson, I was leaving on empty in the area of relationships.

Spiritual retreats are another avenue for women seeking a greater connection. When I looked on the internet for Christian Women's retreats, for example, there were about 160,000 listings. A weekend spiritual retreat can be just as renewing to your personal life as a professional retreat is when you are feeling burned out on the job. Whether through an internet search or with a phone book and a couple of phone calls, you can find out about on-going spiritual enrichment groups, Bible studies, or spiritual retreats for women.

BOOK CLUBS

My friend Louise is in a multicultural book club. I recently saw a mother-daughter book club on TV. I could see this would open the doors of communication between mothers and their teen daughters to talk about really important issues that might otherwise be skirted. Neighborhood book clubs for women have also become increasingly popular; I can't think of a better way to get to know your neighbors. Other small groups can sometimes spin off and develop from your book club. Cindy met a few women in her book club that later agreed to go walking together. Don't fall into the trap of quickly judging or sizing up a group; one person in the group, or one activity of the group, may create a connection to something more meaningful for you.

EVERYTHING ELSE UNDER THE SUN GROUPS

Some women I know belong to an all-female investment group where they pool money and invest in the market. Each person is responsible for researching one stock and they each invest so much per month. If you live in a big city you could locate women from around the world and start a women's multicultural group. We miss out on so much when we close ourselves off from women of other races, cultures, or religions, and unwittingly perpetuate fear and hostility over misunderstood differences.

Every city should have a newcomers group. If you locate such a group (call your local chamber of commerce) you can later form a smaller group with some of the women you met while a newcomer. For those who have a hobby or special interest, like hiking or some type of craft, you can always form a group around that activity. You can also tie your group theme to current events to get started, such as using your craft skills to make a needed item for children in local hospitals or shelters.

JUMP RIGHT IN— JOINING UP OR STARTING YOUR OWN GROUP

Taking Responsibility—Taking Action

If you are not in a women's group two probable reasons are: (1) You don't want to be, or (2) You haven't made it happen. If you don't want to, fine, you're choosing what you want. But if you want to be in a group, you have to take responsibility for either finding and joining an existing one, or starting your own. I would not be enjoying participation in the fun group that I am in if I hadn't stepped forward and asked. I had to be willing to take a risk. You will have to take some risks, too.

Finding an Existing Group

Maybe you're an introvert and wouldn't find it easy to call fifteen people in hopes of getting a group started. You realize you're in a big rut, and now that your kids are zipping around with their friends night and day, you're lonely. You hear about all of the fun that women are having in groups, but you think that you're too bashful or dull, and besides, you can't even name five women that you know well enough to call. And what would you say; you don't even know what kind of group you'd like to start. Maybe you would be more comfortable finding an existing group to join. Begin by turning your thoughts into intentional action. Say out loud that being in a group is what you want, and then be ready to take some risks. What have you got to lose? If it doesn't work, you'll be right back where you started, not a bit worse off.

Now that your thoughts and actions are clear and intentional, you can begin your search for a group that's right for you. What's missing in your life? You may also approach your search with the question, "What do I love to do?" If it's gardening, painting, crafts, or reading, look for a group that shares your interest. Then just pick up the phone and start calling, networking, until you locate what you're looking for. To be a good net worker, don't ever hang up without asking that person if they know who else you might try. Calling libraries, women's resource centers, community centers, YMCAs, or churches could turn up existing groups for spiritual growth, special interest, or physical fitness. Other groups can be located on the internet, and if the group you contact is full, leaders of existing groups will be glad to tell you how to start your own.

Starting Your Own Group

I have a picture of our chapter of the Sweet Potato Queens on the bookshelf in my office. Sometimes women will ask me about it and then begin talking about their need for friends. So often they feel on the outside looking in and believe that they are flawed, because they don't have friends.

Rhonda, a woman that I have seen in therapy for three months, is an introvert who was seriously lacking in confidence. She very much wanted to be in a women's group, but lacked confidence in herself. In one session I had her write down her actual qualities, such as honesty, loyalty, and a willingness to work hard. After reviewing the list of qualities with me, she reluctantly admitted that she would like to have a friend with those qualities. She also had to admit that if *she* would want a friend with those traits, then someone else would probably want a friend like her. She was encouraged to think of *one* person that could be a potential friend. She then agreed to call that one person and talk about some of the women's groups that she's heard about and ask her friend if she would be interested in forming a women's group. Her friend, who turned out to be interested, called two of her friends, who then called their friends. Out of that many women, someone always emerges as a leader, so the bashful introvert doesn't have to worry about being in charge. My client was able to enjoy being a part of a group without feeling the pressure to lead. She did have to be willing to step out of her comfort zone to call that first person, but she didn't have to change who she was.

KEEPING IT TOGETHER—THE GROUP, THAT IS

Creativity and Consistency

Okay, let's say you are successful in either asking yourself into an existing group, or in starting your own. What holds a group together once you get started? Here's what works for our group: regular contact without long intervals of inactivity. We have twelve members in our group and are regularly getting together for everyone's birthday. We keep some other activity in the planning at all times, which then leads to other necessary activities. In the end, it's all about the creativity of women, the ideas they present, and the fun we experience in sharing both.

Our group members also like to surprise each other with little gifts. Two of us made matching tote bags and presented them to the girls before we left on our Jackson trip. Another member bought everyone a hot pink, feathered fan to prevent a sure death from that Mississippi heat and humidity. These identical items provided a visible connection, too. When you see twelve women dressed alike you have no question in your mind that they are a group – a clearly defined group.

Change is Inevitable

All groups will inevitably change, and that's when they might start to fizzle. While we have had enormous fun, we felt compelled to add some "good works" to our repertoire. Here are some tips: Make each person responsible for something, and always keep an event on the calendar to look forward to. We discovered that a willingness to add, take away, or change ideas or activities is necessary. Each time the group meets, it's good to talk about the next activity, meeting, or project. This continuity keeps our mindset as a part of a group, and doesn't leave us wondering if there's something after this.

There must also be a willingness to make friendships a priority, and that sometimes means sacrificing participation in something else in order to maintain the connection. Making new friends isn't really that hard, but maintaining friendships, especially groups, is harder. If you're a group member and miss half of the gatherings, then you will only get half as much out of being part of a group. We can go long periods of time without seeing lifelong friends and usually pick up where we left off, but with new friends, if too much time goes by in between visits, it's almost like starting over.

But What About Gossip?

One of the questions asked when considering a women's group is, "Do women pair up, and doesn't gossip cause problems?" It's inevitable that some members of the group will know each other before the group forms. I have to accept that if some members of the group have been friends since high school, then they will certainly talk more, see each other more, and share at a deeper level. In my younger years this would have bothered me, but as a midlife woman I am more secure now, and I look upon this as an opportunity to become a good friend to all of them. Remember the song we sang when we were kids? "Make new friends, but keep the old. One is silver and the other gold." (We really did learn everything we needed to know in kindergarten!)

The answer to the gossip issue is simpler than you'd think. The members have to intentionally declare that they aren't going to take part in gossip. If everybody wants to be part of a group, then they will have to acknowledge that it won't work if there's gossip in it. Talk about it together as a preventative measure; it will make each member more likely to be accountable. If gossip is never talked about, then someone's flaw may get the best of them. Just be responsible for yourself in this area; if someone approaches you with gossip, don't let it go any farther. It takes at least two to make it continue.

DO I HAVE TO STRIP NAKED AND DRINK TEQUILA FROM THE BOTTLE?
Doing What's Comfortable

Everything's relative. When I talk about women getting in touch with their "wild side," I'm not talking about going topless or drinking contests. We are looking for some of that lost adolescent freedom and pure fun, and for most of us midlifers that means just doing something non-productive and silly. "Wild" for the average American middle-aged woman may mean not cooking dinner for the family in order to meet her friends at a respectable restaurant where she may have one of those gigantic frozen margaritas.

Although I feel free to be me in the group, I don't expect anyone in the group who isn't comfortable with an activity that I consider fun to feel obligated to participate. When we go on road trips there are some activities that I don't want to participate in, and my group is quite okay with that. It's very important as you go along to sort out your own comfort level.

Be Willing To Try New Things

If you always do the same thing, you'll always get the same thing…so why not branch out a little? I'm not suggesting you do anything that feels wrong, but you might do something you wish you could do if you had the guts. In other words, don't say "no" just because it's something you've never done before. Moving up a few notches on the "wildness" scale, our group decided to have a pajama party. We all brought snacks (mostly chocolate), and some of our more degenerate members supplied margaritas. We danced to loud music and later sat in the hot tub under the stars talking about whatever was on our minds. We then put on our pajamas and piled up with pillows in cushy chairs and sofas to watch "girl" movies.

Trips—Opportunities for Bonding

True bonding (and the most fun) takes place on road trips. When you're in the car for six hours, or you're sharing a hotel room with friends, you certainly get to know each other. Our group has made several road trips—to Jackson, Mississippi, to the beach, to see the Jackie

Kennedy exhibit in Washington, D. C. , to New Orleans, and to Nashville. We are now planning a spring trip to Savannah, Georgia. Since all twelve of us can't make every trip, the makeup of each excursion is different.

QUESTIONS AND SUGGESTIONS

Question: If you are not already part of a women's group, would you like to be?
Suggestion: Write down the many types of groups talked about in this chapter. (For instance:groups just for fun, health and fitness, book clubs, spiritual growth, etc.)Now rate from one to ten each category according to your own preference, or need. If you feel out of shape, you may rate "fitness" with an "eight." If you already have intellectual stimulation, you may rate "book club" with a "three." The highest number will tell you where you currently have the biggest need. Now write that group at the top of a new page.

Question: Do you know of existing groups where you might get this identified area of need or interest met? If not, do you know someone (a neighbor who is well connected) who might know?
Suggestion: Network with that neighbor or friend regarding this identified category. At the end of the conversation, ask who else you might call to get more information, and continue doing that until you are satisfied with the information you have. Call one place or organization that might offer that type of group. For instance, if it's reading that interests you, call Barnes and Noble bookstore and ask about open book clubs. If it is spiritual growth you desire, call your local church or synagogue. Write the information you get from each call under the group topic you chose. Now choose a group and try it!

Question: If you are unable to find an existing group to join, are you willing to take risks and the required action to start you own?
Suggestion: If you answered yes, write down one woman's name from each of the following categories:church or synagogue, neighborhood, workplace, parents of your children's friends, existing girlfriends, or acquaintances who are potential friends. Start at the top of your list and call each woman to ask about her interest and willingness to participate. Don't forget about networking. Even if a woman doesn't share that particular need at this time, she might know someone who does. If she is interested, ask her to call one other person, and so on, until the group is filled.

7

Finding Your Passion—What Passion?

I used to get so frustrated when I watched those television shows about "finding your passion" or "following your dream." I didn't feel any passion, and most of my dreams involved being chased by weird-looking monsters. I remember lying on the couch and searching every cell in my brain for that hidden passion, that dream that was hiding or that surely I'd forgotten. I tried, but I couldn't squeeze that dream out, yet people kept telling me I just simply had to follow it.

I could think of about three people I knew personally who had "dreams," and they all had exceptional talent. You know the kind—they had eighteen years of dance lessons or they could play Mozart by the time they were three. These gifted people didn't have to lay awake at night wondering what direction they would take; they always knew because their talent drove them. So what about the ordinary people whose talents aren't quite so obvious?

Women in their forties and fifties, freed up by the empty nest, are not only actively searching for their true selves, but they are searching to recapture some of the passion that once drove them in their youth. But the search for "passion" is a puzzle to most women, and many might just skim right over this part of their lives. It's hard to tell someone else how to find their dream, because it is something hiding deep inside of each individual. However, there are things that you can do to help coax your dreams and passions from their hiding place, making it easier for you to see and experience them. Before you begin your search, you will find it helpful to understand why dreams and passions are hiding, missing, or going unnoticed in the first place.

WHERE DID I LOSE IT...MY DREAMS, MY PASSION?

Robbed From the Cradle

Some of us hardly got out of the cradle before we were robbed of our tiny seeds of interest that could have developed into life-fulfilling passions. It was rarely done on purpose, but nonetheless, people and events in our lives helped to turn our heads in different directions than they might have been naturally inclined to turn. I was shopping the other day when I heard a father say to his son, "Put that down, it's not for boys; boys can't play with that." I turned around and saw a boy, about four years old, holding a large, bright pink toy. He seemed determined to have it, but his father was bigger and more determined. I don't remember exactly what the toy was, but it struck me how our natural choices and inclinations in early childhood are rewarded only if they match our parent's (or other adults in authority) approval.

There are plenty of environmental circumstances that can also contribute to stifling interests in children. Julie, a thirty-four-year-old client who was addicted to prescription drugs, grew up in a chaotic environment with abusive parents, who moved her from town to town and school to school. Not only were the adults in her life incapable of nurturing and supporting her with the basics (food, transportation, safety, etc.), but they were certainly not able to recognize and nurture any special interests she may have had. Now, as an adult, she can't remember anything about her childhood years except her strong fear, which blossomed into anger in her adolescence.

Even positive stress, stress that comes from good events or changes, can prevent our interests from developing into passion. A child can be getting a lot of positive feedback and reward for something, keeping them focused on that one goal, while some other seed of interest may go ignored by adults and eventually abandoned by the child. In other words, the behavior that is rewarded and reinforced by adults is the one the child will more likely stick with. I got a lot of attention for making good grades in my youth, but my interest in art, dancing, and dramatics was pretty much ignored by my parents. I moved further away from these creative fields of interest and focused more on the areas that got me positive attention from my parents.

Parents may be guilty of pushing children and taking actions that are contrary to the child's nature. Legendary actress Natalie Wood was pushed by her mother to fulfill her mother's dreams, not her own. She was told by her mother at a very young age that she must be a movie star. In her twenties, Natalie would complain of feeling fake, not knowing who she really was, yet she was on an outwardly successful path. But outward success is not the same as feeling successful on the inside. We all know people who make a lot of money, but absolutely hate what they do.

Remember the Fairy Tale?

Elizabeth Berg in her book *The Pull of the Moon* tells the story of a woman, married twenty-five years, who "runs away from home" in search of her true self. She recalls her confidence and belief in herself as a girl. "I believed, at twelve, that I could be a scientist. I read a book a day. I believed I could be a writer, an actress, a professor of English in Rome, an acrobat in a purple-spangled outfit...my life was like a wild, beating thing, exotic, capable of unfolding and enlarging itself, pulling itself higher and higher up like a kite loved by the wind. . . There in front of me, my own for the taking. And then, suddenly, lost."

Most women start out with this kind of hope and belief in themselves, but, unlike men, become so caught up in the fantasy of being rescued (by a male) that they leave their own dreams behind. From the time they fixated on boys, women were no longer dreaming their own dreams, but were focusing on all things, tangible and intangible, that men might provide for them. Most of us did *dream* we'd get married, didn't we? And why did most of us, even those of us who were never meant to reside with another human being, dream of marriage? It all comes back to the fairy tale, the fantasy of the rescue by Prince Charming, and the promise of the "happily ever after." Men, on the other hand, were socialized to focus on their own personal pursuits.

The fairy tale not only robbed women of their own dreams and passions, but set men up for a shocker. Think how a man must feel, when after much hard work, he succeeds at being a very charming "prince" only to have his midlife wife in crisis because she's unhappy with *her* life. How disarming it must be for men who unwittingly bought into their role of the fairy tale rescue. Yes, he heard the fairy tales too, and he, like you, expected *you* to be happy and fulfilled just being with him. Men may have created the fairy tale, but it definitely backfired on them. They face disillusionment as well when faced with women who want more.

Caught in Someone Else's Dream

Illusions about the fairy tale took you off track, and before you knew it, you were living someone else's dream. The romance made it easy to put your dreams aside in order to focus on his. After all, isn't that what you were supposed to do? Women didn't just sacrifice career success for their men, they also stopped pursuing other areas of self fulfillment or pleasure. The ingrained rules of patriarchy prompted us to step back if our own needs, dreams, and desires inconvenienced our husband in any way. I'm speaking in the past tense, but in reality, many women still feel this way today. Even those of us who consider ourselves "liberated" will admit to still feeling that we are caught up in someone else's life. Every place that I have lived since I got married was chosen because of a career decision my husband made. Whether we watched TV, or read at night, was based on his schedule. This revelation hit me a few months ago while I was enjoying a relaxing evening of late- night television alone, all snuggled up on the sofa. I was switching between Jay Leno and David Letterman (the thrill of holding the remote was exhilarating!). My son and husband were in bed and the house was beautifully quiet. Suddenly I looked up and saw my husband standing there in the doorway, his face twisted into a sleepy question mark. When I didn't respond, he asked me if I knew what time it was, and when would I be coming to bed? Then it hit me: I was a middle-aged woman being chastised for staying up past my bed time!

Actually, I'm a night owl who went to bed early because my husband did. It may sound silly, but going to bed when I feel like going to bed is now one of those little things that I do that makes me feel more like I'm living my own life. Many women are realizing how little of their lives they live on their own terms. We don't want to become self-centered, but we could surely become more balanced in this area.

Too Busy With Life to Really Live it

So we followed the fairy tale and got caught up in *his* dream. Why is it so hard to recapture *our* dreams once we let them go? Well, it's mostly because we're just too busy and moving too fast. Constant activity blocks out the inner voice; it's now just a thin whisper and most of us have far too much noise in our lives for it to be heard. Once we make a home with someone else, having romanticized dreams about *his* role in *our* happiness, we are then caught up in the details of living it out. In other words, once we have chosen a direction, right or wrong, our energies go into getting there. It's entirely possible to be married and follow your dreams, but it won't happen if you let go of them during the romance.

Once I let go of my graduate school admission in order to move to Nebraska for my husband's career, the direction was chosen, and a chain of events followed that kept me *busy* for many years. I could have stayed and finished my graduate work. I could have put off having children for two more years. I could have held on to my dream, but I let it go. Then I got so busy in the chain of events that followed that I quit thinking about it at all…until I was almost forty. Midlife restlessness is a wonderful thing.

Women who get so busy that their dreams are lost in the shuffle may become hostile and develop resentment toward their spouses. Their time and their energies focus on their husband's success instead of their own. My mother is a prime example; she never pursued her own dreams of becoming a professional singer, but she was always slightly angry at my father for not being more successful. Women often project their desire for success onto men, then develop unfair expectations of them. These high expectations that are displaced onto men may then go unmet, leaving women resentful. A man, feeling his partner's disappointment, may react by distancing himself, returning the hostility, or getting involved with a younger woman who still believes in the fairy tale and dreamily thinks that he's her answer to the good life.

CREATING THE RIGHT ENVIRONMENT
Taking the Reins

Now that you have taken the time to review your early years and the things that distracted you from your personal dreams, you are ready to begin the search for your own hidden passion. Even if you can't remember having any dreams, you can develop some new dreams and begin to seek out something in life that you can feel passionate about. Maybe when you were a little girl, you longed to be a movie star. But you're forty-six now and, let's face it, that's a tough dream. In reality, you are probably not going to be the next great actress, but you could be the best thing that ever happened to your community theater.

"But I wasn't ever in the school play; in fact, I wasn't really very good at anything," you may say. What you're truly saying is, "I never became *aware* of my strengths." Whether your dreams were stifled, pushed off track, or never made aware to you in the first place, you can still begin the search. Start by creating the right environment for a successful search. You are now in control, not pushed or hindered by parents, no longer dreaming someone else's dream; it's up to you and you can do it. If *you've* given up control to another person, *you* have to take it back. You're a big girl now and you don't believe in fairy tales.

The Power of Intent

We tend to be what we intend to be. Our intent determines the choices we make from moment to moment. Do you intend to be a victim of your youthful mistakes, or do you intend to be the best you can be with what you know *now*? I can't take back one single thing that I did because of stupidity or immaturity, but I can certainly make new choices with new intentions that take me to a new place now.

It's hard to tell someone how to find her dream, and that's probably why it takes so long and why so few of us get there. We can't give somebody a recipe for a foolproof method, but we can certainly pass along the conditions which must be met in order for others to even make it a possibility. You must first allow yourself to want it, be intent on having it. Dare to long for a dream of your own; be hungry for a passion that drives you and open yourself up to it. You must accept that you can't force it, but vow to do whatever it takes to create the right environment.

It would be easy to get off track here with dreams and expectations of fame or wealth; that's another story. Most famous or wealthy people will tell you that they took risks to pursue something they loved. They followed their hearts, not dollar signs, for purpose and meaning. Because they were good at what they loved, gave it their best, and maybe were in the right place at the right time, they got famous, wealthy, or both. Most will agree that they didn't start on their journey with money or fame as the goal. A *conscious* decision to find a life of passion and purpose must be made; a person doesn't just drift into it from some place. Your search for a purpose, a dream, and a life of passion must be *intentional.*

That Congruency Thing...Again

The next step toward an active search for your passion involves an internal "check-up" for congruency. I have talked about finding your true self, which requires matching up your knowledge, your words, and your actions. How can you have legitimate dreams and feel genuine passion for something if you aren't really being "you?" How can you know yourself if you're talking or acting like somebody else? You're likely to dredge up somebody else's dream if you don't yet know yourself. Women who continue to please others must first locate their own inner voice and find their true selves before they can find their true purposes. They must learn how to identify their own wants, needs, and desires and then learn how to assert those needs.

Many women tell me that they have a hard time remembering and reinstituting their own values and beliefs into their changed lives. When you have built a life around somebody else's beliefs, it may take some doing to get down to the core of your own. There is no internal conflict when all parts of us match up, and in this state of peace, you can have the energy and focus you need to look inward. Once you have become a congruent person you are more able to open up and realize your own dreams and desires. Now that you've got your innards in order, you'll probably need to make a few adjustments to your external environment.

Solitude

Remember when life wasn't so complicated? There was a thing called solitude, but you were probably too young to appreciate it back then. Nowadays, solitude means sitting on the toilet for five minutes without the phone ringing. Our work, families, and daily chores keep us spinning like a wheel, and our lives are more cluttered than ever before. We have lost the art of solitude. Today we are dealing with constant distractions so solitude must be a purposeful, planned activity. In solitude, when there are no distractions, your mind is free to create new ideas, and in this stillness, your spirit can speak to you purposefully and sincerely. Arranging time for solitude may require you to simplify and let go of less meaningful activities. This has been extremely hard for me.

Solitude is quite uncomfortable at first, particularly for those who haven't experienced it in a while, but the benefits are astounding. I love what Anne Morrow Lindbergh said in her book, *Gifts From The Sea*, when referring to getting in touch with herself through solitude at the beach. "When one is a stranger to oneself then one is estranged from others too. If one is out of touch with oneself, then one cannot touch others." I rarely hear women say that they have gone to the beach alone, or traveled to the mountains alone; we spend very little time alone these days. Some women don't even know how to be alone; they panic when no one is around. We can also better appreciate other people in our lives when we have some time separate from them. When I get away, whether by myself or with friends, I am always more appreciative of my family when I return. I have been fortunate enough to have a husband who has supported my need for solitude and has inconvenienced himself while I retreat. We all need some space in order to see ourselves as we truly are—separate, unique individuals. We come into this world alone, and we leave this world alone. I am learning to embrace, not fear, solitude.

THE ACTIVE SEARCH
Allowing Yourself to Dream It

Once you create the environment of openness and state your intent, summon your dreams and let your thoughts flow freely. Dream things that don't seem possible. Pearl S. Buck wrote, "The young do not know enough to be prudent, and therefore they attempt the impossible – and achieve it, generation after generation." You must be willing to entertain "crazy," seemingly impossible ideas. And, when I say "entertain," I mean entertain your thoughts like a southern girl is taught to entertain her guests. You must invite those thoughts to sit for a while, make them more comfortable, and pour a tall glass of iced tea while you engage them; you mustn't rush them along.

Once you find a quiet place where you can be alone, your thoughts will move freely through your mind. Don't dismiss any at first. Don't get into the habit of squelching ideas before they can develop into dreams. Critiquing your thoughts too quickly and labeling ideas as impossible will keep you from ever knowing the possibilities…your possibilities.

Many successful women will tell you that five years ago they would have never believed or dared to dream of the successes they experience today. But once they started to visualize their own successes, they were able to identify the first step in getting there. You have to intentionally visualize yourself accessing all you need in order to be what you dream of being. And when you are visualizing, don't put limits on what you will think or dream about. For instance, don't get hung up thinking that you have to limit your dreams to the various ways in which you can earn a living. Your real passion—ministry, gardening, political campaigning, gourmet cooking, painting, decorating, or crafting— may be enjoyed on your days off. If I limit my dreams to any certain category or put restrictions on my flow of ideas, then I may miss the point and never find my true passion in life.

There may be more than one way to fulfill your passion and bring happiness into your life; you may find purpose and meaning in more than one arena. For instance, if I feel passionate about women's issues, and I am concerned by their lack of self confidence and assertiveness, I could channel this in any number of directions. I could work directly with women teaching them skills. I could serve on the board of an agency that empowers women. I could volunteer at a battered women's shelter. I could write a book that empowers women. One passion can flow into many channels. Once you are empowered, your energy flows wherever it is directed.

Ask yourself this question, "What makes me smile, excited, sit up a little straighter, or feel strong emotion?" Maybe you get emotional when you hear about the downtrodden, weak, or abused. Maybe you get excited when a chef comes on a television show and starts talking about creative cooking. Maybe you get passionate about the poor quality of education in some of our schools, or the lack of resources for children with special needs. It's not always so simple, but pay attention, because it is a clue, a piece of the puzzle. Subjects that arouse emotions in us give us clues to where our passions lie.

Don't be afraid to ask your friends or people that you work with where they think your strengths lie. Ask your children or other supportive family members what they think you are good at, care about, or get excited about. Reflect on your youth, your school days; what were you interested in then? There are always clues out there, and it's in your best interest to search them out.

Dare to Say It

Saying it is the next step after dreaming it and visualizing it. Of course, you won't feel certain that you can accomplish it, and that is okay; you are just in the beginning stages. When a flash of "light" comes through your brain, say it out loud. I remember when I first said out loud that I was going to write a book. What if I couldn't accomplish it? What if it was a flop? It takes courage to say out loud what you dream, what you want. I'm also more likely to do it now that I've said it out loud. When I said it to my friends, they acted like they believed in me (whether they did or not), and that helped me believe in myself. Yes, it's risky, and yes, there's no certainty of success. Everything in life is uncertain. I'm either going to be paralyzed, or I will move forward in spite of uncertainty.

Once you have voiced your dream, you may benefit from feedback or gain ideas and momentum from others who want to see you succeed. Most things are easier when shared. Be careful not to let yourself become discouraged if some people react negatively – that is most likely about them, not you.

Once we are intentional about doing what we feel passionate about, we must say it before we lose our nerve. Once your passion is spoken, it becomes more real and has to be acted upon. If you say, "I haven't got anybody to tell, nobody that I trust to whom I could confide something so personal," then you need to reread Chapter Five and renew your commitment to find some women friends. Just one will do, for now.

Write It Down

It is therefore my contention that dreams, ideas, or fantasies of accomplishment, still pop into our consciousness from time to time but we have learned to squash those little flashes of enlightenment before they can develop into real intentional thought. So, instead of sitting down and trying to force thoughts about how you can find significance in life, just promise yourself that you will not squelch any random thoughts or dreams when they happen by. Your dreams and passions are summoned in this way and you will find them appearing in the mist of other activities.

If a television show stimulates a dream or fantasy of writing a children's book, opening a shop, or becoming a missionary, turn the television off, think about it for a while, then *write down* your thoughts, no matter how outrageous they seem at the time.

Even more powerful than the spoken intent is the written intention. As soon as you can say what you dream about, you must write it down. I often tell my clients to write in a journal because there's something very powerful about seeing their thoughts on paper. Ideas can float around forever, get muddled, or be quickly forgotten if they stay in our heads. Putting them down on paper is a way to give them more weight. When I write down an idea, it often leads to another idea; then I can track a train of thought.

Simple Beginnings

Start out very simply, with tiny steps, not giant steps. Remember: Your dreams need to be BIG, but your steps need to be small. You have dared to dream of being a great decorator. You have told your family and friends about your dream and you have written it down on paper. It's a big dream, but take a small first step; call the nearest college with an interior design department and simply ask for an appointment to talk to someone about their program and the field of decorating in general. Your next step is small too: show up for your appointment, on time, bringing an open mind and a pad and a pencil. Big steps are overwhelming; little steps are easy...and *simple.*

The biggest mistake we make in thinking of change or reaching a goal is to focus too far out into the future. In therapy, clients come into my office feeling anxious and overwhelmed, realizing their need for change. They can see the final result, the changed person, and become quickly overwhelmed thinking about *everything* that needs to be done to get there. Helping them see just the next step and focus on it alone will get them moving in the right direction. A race is won through a series of steps, not a jump to the finish line.

Alcoholics Anonymous teaches a person who is committed to breaking a bad addiction to take one day at a time. If a person has been relying for years on alcohol to soothe their bad feelings, the idea of being alcohol free can be overwhelming and cause so much anxiety that the person may feel the urge to drink. But if that person says to herself, "I can get through *this one day* without using alcohol to numb my feelings," then she is likely to succeed and reach that small step toward her big goal.

Julie, one woman to whom I spoke, had a husband with terminal cancer. I felt that anything I said would be inadequate, so I just asked her how she was doing. "Well, she said, "We are just focusing on doing the next thing." Terminal cancer in someone you love is an overwhelming sorrow. But she was managing her feelings by keeping her focus on just the one step ahead. If chemotherapy was scheduled, then she focused on what she needed to do to get her husband and herself through that experience. I've often thought about the wisdom in her response. Instead of letting a tremendous problem overtake her, she instead put her force into taking this one simple step forward.

FIGHTING THE FEAR
Taking Risks

Famed author and humorist Erma Bombeck said, "There are people who put their dreams in a little box and say, 'Yes, I've got dreams, of course, I've got dreams.' Then they put the box away and bring it out once in a while to look in it, and yep, they're still there. These are great dreams, but they never even get out of the box. It takes an uncommon amount of guts to put your dreams on the line, to hold them up and say, how good or how bad am I? That's where courage comes in."

To find our passion we can't sit at home waiting for strength to appear at the door like the pizza delivery man. Happiness doesn't come with home delivery; you have to get in the driver's seat and go out in the rain after it. Contentment comes from the fulfillment we experience when our dreams are being lived out, not just thought about. Most of the really good stuff in life requires intentional, purposeful action on our part. And to get the really good stuff in life, you are required to take risks. Keeping your dreams in a box is nice and safe, but only when you *live* that dream will you feel fully alive and make that dream a reality.

"What if?" Thinking

What if I go after my dream and I fail? What if I produce a thousand specialty T-shirts and no one buys them? What if I invest all of that time and energy into writing a short story and then find out I don't really like it? These are worry statements that create anxiety, not confidence. Try turning them around. What if I go after my dream and succeed? What if I sell thousands of T-shirts? What if I find out I love writing more than anything I could have imagined? Then you might ask yourself, "What will happen if I sit here and never take a chance?"

As a child you could see yourself doing or being something great in the future; those thoughts just popped into your head. You might have had a flash where you saw yourself as a famous ballerina or even the President of the United States. If you were anything like me, you dreamed on it for a while, picturing yourself performing perfectly before an adoring audience. You didn't stop to think of all the "what ifs" when you were eight or nine; you just went with it, allowing yourself to feel and experience what it would be like to be a success.

As adults, the "what if" thinking generally trips us up before our daydream even gets rolling. We may start "what iffing" before we even understand the source or passion behind an idea that flashes into our mind. When we squelch dreams with "what if" thinking, we may blind ourselves to the possibilities before they even have time to be revealed. Some would say it is fear of failure and some would theorize it is fear of success. I say the *content* of the fear is irrelevant; it's all about fear that bad things *might* happen, and giving in to that fear. Fear paralyzes us and keeps us from moving forward or backwards.

However, there is a major problem in thinking, "I'll lose the fear and then I'll take a step." It just doesn't work that way. I must take a step, see that I survived it, and watch a little of the fear slip away. I'm still shaky, but since I survived the last step, I might as well take another. Low and behold, I survived again and now I have a bit of confidence to take another step. I take one more step, and so on and so on. This is where confidence comes from—one shaky, fear-filled step at a time. So we're talking about not waiting for fear to subside in order to act, but acting *in spite of* fear.

Getting the Guts

Some of you may have even gone after dreams and failed, and now have to muster up the courage to try again. Many of the accomplished women that I read about, met or worked with, failed multiple times before they enjoyed the satisfaction of success. It was their courage to persist that finally made it happen. Most said that had it not been for the failures, they would not have found their way to the joys they now experience. You must either live a limited life of safety or a fuller life filled with risks. If you choose the full life, you will need the guts to endure some failure along the way. You must accept failure as part of the life experience; it toughens you and makes you even hungrier for success in the right place and at the right time.

Don't mistake an obstacle for a failure. If you're quick to give up when an obstacle arrives, then you'll be sure to miss the opportunity to succeed. If you stop and figure out a way around the obstacle, then you can still continue on your journey. Obstacles that appear in our path can actually enable us to be more creative than before. Don't be afraid or immediately put a negative meaning when you encounter an obstacle; think of it as a sign that you need to learn more so that you can do better. People who are focused on doing better become better at what they want to do.

Stepping Out – of Your Rut, That Is

Stepping out of your own comfort zone will set the stage for new experiences, new people, and new ideas to enter your life. There is no inspiration in a rut, so get out. If you aren't getting inspiration doing your daily routine, then you must get out of your routine to find it. You can read new books or articles, talk to more people about different things, or visit places you don't normally go. You must get out of your rut in order to form a new groove. So accept the necessity of risks, overcome the "what ifs," get some guts, and take that first shaky step out of your personal rut.

If you've been lacking in courage, paralyzed, and stuck in a rut due to fear, how will you begin to find the courage to change? Like anything else that you want, you first have to identify the need and make time for it. Identify fear as the real reason you're not stepping out to get what you want. Then make a commitment to change, and make a plan as to how you will overcome your fear of new people, places, or experiences by facing that fear one step, one new experience, at a time. If your fear is in the form of persistent, excessive worry, then you may benefit from seeing a professional counselor in order to develop a strategy for overcoming it. Otherwise, if you're just cowardly, heal thyself. Take a deep breath, swallow, and walk your first step forward.

Observable, Measurable Behaviors

After you identify the need, in this case, courage, then define the behaviors associated with that quality. In other words, ask yourself how a person having courage would behave. What is a person with courage doing that you're not doing? What would a person with courage do to take this one simple step toward their goal? Stay away from global terms like, "I would be brave." Describe a brave or courageous person in *behavioral* terms that can be observed and measured (as to whether it's happening or not, and how much it's happening).

You might note, for instance, that a person with courage would pick up the phone and risk rejection in order to ask for that interview. She would risk rejection in order to ask others for assistance. A courageous person would risk failure in order to commit to a leadership role on a committee. A courageous person would risk looking "stupid" in order to try something they've never done before. Get the picture? As you face each step in your journey to pursue your dream, ask yourself what a person with courage would do. Then, do that thing yourself; the repeated acts of doing or *behaving* like a courageous person will lead you to *becoming* a courageous person. We behave our way to being the person we want to be.

MY STORY

I have been a social worker for thirty years, and during that time have worked with children, youth, adults, and the elderly. Currently, in my private practice, I work mainly with women of varied ages, many of whom are in distress caused by problems in their relationships with men. Many of these women lack confidence. Working with these particular clients has made me feel more alive, energetic, and significant. Helping these women learn assertiveness, find congruency, and gain confidence inspires me. Through my passion with this work came my desire to write this book.

When I told my husband that I was writing a book on women gaining courage and finding their life purposes, I really wasn't certain that I could actually do it or get it published. I did know, however, that I would learn a lot along the way and meet a lot of wonderful women in the process. I knew that writing my thoughts down and talking with other women about things that I felt passionate about could only help me find clarity about myself and my beliefs. "If this betters me, then I haven't lost a thing by taking the risk and giving myself to it." You, too, have nothing to lose if the risks you take and what you do improves you in some way.

I mentioned earlier how I happened to become part of a women's "sweet potato queen" group. I was longing for friends, willing to meet new people and do new things. When asked to travel ten hours to Jackson, Mississippi, for the annual St. Patrick's Day Parade, my first thought was that I was too busy. However, I was highly motivated to gather with other women like myself, so I went. While in Jackson, I became very impressed with the creativity, energy, warmth, and amazing feats of the hundreds of women present. There were inspiring stories about women fighting devastating odds, such as cancer, and other women supporting them and coming to their aid. I was hearing this message of empowerment, one that I wanted so badly to relate to the women I see in my office. I was hearing something that reinforced a passion already there. By giving myself this new experience, however, the passion was stirred, so much so that I was able to clearly recognize it. Had I let my busy life keep me home, I would have missed the boat.

I was high with the energy that permeated that crowd and that night on the ride home we talked about women's issues for ten hours straight. Upon returning home, I couldn't sleep, and sometime during the early morning hours, I knew that I had to write a book about a subject that was now close to my heart. The subject of empowerment for women causes my heart to pump a little faster; it energizes me. I discovered my passion because I created the environment to allow dreams to happen. I took a risk, got out of my rut, and took action.

You have by now accepted responsibility for where you find yourself; you desire change and you know it's up to you. You are self-caring and nurture your mind, body, and spirit. You are patient, understanding that this change takes time. You create an environment that allows your passion to bubble up and reveal itself. As a result, you find a real live dream, a vision of purpose, something that excites you and makes you feel significant. What's next? How does one go about life any differently once she discovers her passion? Wasn't I already working in an area that I was passionate about when I was counseling women who lacked confidence and empowerment? Wasn't I already living my dream?

I was involved in an activity that was part of the environment needed for discovery. I certainly did enjoy providing guidance to women struggling to find their way, but I had not yet *recognized* the full reach of my passion for these women's issues until I added new experiences, like becoming part of a women's group and making the trip to Jackson. That experience with hundreds of other women triggered a light that came on and allowed me to see more of what was already there. Being willing to open yourself up to new experiences, people, or ideas, is essential in discovering your passions that lie beneath the surface.

TURNING DREAMS INTO GOLD...I MEAN GOALS

Three different people may have a passion for flowers, but they all won't have a burning desire to open up a flower shop. One may dream of having the loveliest garden, another may enjoy creating artistic floral arrangements, and the third may envision having a quaint little shop that specializes in tropical flowers. The same passion—but three different goals. Finding your passion is just the first part; setting specific goals to put your passion into action is the second part.

Let's look at the third lover of flowers. As long as she's fantasizing about having that cute little shop some day, it remains a dream. As soon as her thoughts become intentional and she lays out a plan of action, then it becomes her goal. Dreams remain dreams until we add *action*.

Remember Erma Bombeck's comments about keeping your dreams locked up in a little box? Some people tell me that they have always dreamed of writing a book. As soon as the idea of writing a book for women popped into my head, I felt compelled to do it. I immediately took action with simple steps. I bought two notebooks, several organizers, and a laptop. I planned regular meetings at the bookstore with a friend, who was also writing, to discuss and critique each other's work. I took a few baby steps to begin my journey.

Most dreams turn into hard work if they're going to amount to anything. I love reading the stories about women who have struggled to become successful. I recently read about an author whose book sold two million copies, but only after being rejected by the first twenty publishers that looked at it. It would be so easy to give up after twenty rejections; it would be so easy to tell yourself that you're just not good enough. Sometimes we convince ourselves that if there are roadblocks, if it's really hard, then it wasn't meant to be. Confidence comes from doing things that are hard.

QUESTIONS AND SUGGESTIONS

Question: As a child, did you have talents, areas of interest, or dreams about your future?

Suggestion: This exercise shouldn't be done unless you have at least twenty to thirty minutes of quiet time. You need to be undisturbed as you sit quietly, all alone, to conjure up memories tucked away in your childhood. Close your eyes and picture yourself playing, going back as far as you can. Were you playing alone or with someone? What are you playing? Write down at least five such memories, always identifying what you are playing and the role you took. Now try to remember early fantasies about what you would be when you grew up. If you remember any such very early dreams, write them down, no matter how silly they seem. Now jump ahead to about age thirteen or fourteen. Can you recall what you answered when asked by adults, "What do you want to be when you grow up?" Did you have to write any papers in school about that very subject. After you have written down all such memories, look for a theme in these memories. This may serve as a clue to buried desires. Don't panic if you don't see such a pattern. You can begin dreaming at any stage of life!

Question: Do you feel caught in someone else's dream, pulled away from or lacking your own?
Suggestion: Think about the people and circumstances that influenced you to change the purpose or direction that you had intended or dreamed about. Now, think about your actions that allowed this to happen. Write down your current intention in a clear, concise statement. Do you intend to reinstate plans that were abandoned? Do you intend to open yourself up to different places, people, and experiences in hopes of finding a new dream? Writing down your intentions will help clarify the next step, where you write out actions leading to your intended goal.

Question: Are you willing to do what it takes to create the environment for hidden passion or dreams to come to light?
Suggestion: Begin with your statement of intent. Schedule a time for solitude and explore your thoughts regarding purpose and meaning in your life. Use this time to identify three things that you will do to get out of your rut. Write specific actions you will take, such as attending a group activity that you usually ignore, visiting a neighbor that you don't know, driving by the community college to pick up a calendar or catalog, calling the local women's resource center to be put on the mailing list for their newsletter…anything that is not ordinary for you and exposes you to new people and ideas.

8

Finding Your Faith—Rekindling Your Spirit

The Spirit World

I know we don't all define "spirit" in the same way, but I want to share with you my belief that "spirit" is the God-given force inside the human body that is our vital essence. I accept as true that we are more than mind and body; we are spiritual beings. And if I am a spiritual being, then there is a spirit world out there that involves more than shopping and eating, or feeding the intellect. Shopping is fun, eating is good, and learning is great, but they all neglect to feed the spirit. Perhaps my belief can inspire your own and you too will be renewed as I have been.

I believe my spirit can be in communion with my maker and be empowered by that relationship. My spirit can be whole; it can be broken; it can be neglected. It is the part of me that feels hunger when not fed. I feel there is a real rescue available for the lost or wandering spirit is by its creator. But even if God "rescues" us, He doesn't magically provide us with a happy ever after; I believe He does, however, empower us for the job.

Women who get caught up in "giving up and giving in" in order to keep someone else happy may discover that they lose more than the "self" they once knew…they lose their faith. Although a successful midlife crisis or turning point may prompt these women to again listen to that small voice inside rather than to people on the outside, that voice may be quite weak, afraid, confused, ineffective, or just plain lost. The dead or weakened spirit needs to get plugged into its original power source; it needs a connection with its creator. But how can faith never found be discovered or how can a spirit be rekindled if the fire was blown out years ago?

Some young women gave away their faith when they gave away pieces of themselves. Some younger women have never discovered (or uncovered) their faith; it is my hope that those desiring to be their authentic selves will, at the end of their search, find themselves tending to their spirit. No one has a purer vision of your true self than God. And if we believe we are made by an all-powerful and loving God, we must never view ourselves as "less than."

Recipes for Living

It is easy to talk about faith, but it becomes more difficult and less politically correct to talk about the source, the essence, and the mechanics of that faith. I believe that we were created by God and then left with instructions for living in a world that He created. I truly feel that the scripture is the inspired Word of God, given to us to use like a "cookbook" in the kitchen of life. If I don't know the "recipe," then I may start out with the wrong ingredients and not be satisfied with the outcome.

I also believe the Bible is more than just an instruction manual. It speaks not only to our ears, but to our hearts, confirming and affirming an inner consciousness of who God intends or wills us to be. The scriptures tell us that Christ was the Word made into flesh, so therefore we know God by knowing the Word. To my way of thinking, we can't live a life of faith and ignore the Word or His voice.

BUT AREN'T CHRISTIANS SUPPOSED TO BE *SELFLESS?*

I've been talking a lot about finding your true self, focusing on self, and doing what is in your best interest. On the surface that might seem to be contradictory to the selfless philosophy heard about in Sunday schools and churches. However, when I encourage you to focus on your "self," I am discouraging you from making decisions based on what somebody else says, thinks, or believes instead of what you *know* to be true and right for you. If you have been concentrating on simply trying to please or fix others, you know by now that it just doesn't work. I believe you must not allow your life to be guided by outside voices but instead by the voice within.

Doing for Myself versus Doing for Others

When the faith life is referred to as "selfless," I feel it simply means that God has entered the "self" and is now influencing our choices and our desires. Although a woman of faith is no longer "selfish" or self-centered, it doesn't mean that she no longer takes care of herself. She will be self-caring in that she uses her knowledge of his word to do what is right for her. The self-caring woman is concerned with making "right" choices. She is now taking into account God's desires for her.

If I want a God-given purpose, I need to have my own spirit healed and filled; I must allow God to fix me first. On an airplane the flight attendant will instruct you to put on your own oxygen mask before you take care of your children should the cabin lose air pressure. Likewise, without our own spiritual air supply, we won't be much help to those around us who are in need. By filling our spiritual void, we give ourselves the essential ingredients to plan and execute the rest of our life journey.

Doing What is in My Own Best Interest

Doing what is in my best interest sounds selfish. How does that play out for a woman of faith? If I am true to myself by sticking to my faith despite disapproval from others, I will become involved in doing for others. Christ was a great example here; he was never deterred by ridicule or opinions of others; he stuck to his God-given knowledge about what he was here on earth to do. He was given the power to complete that job because he listened to God's voice and submitted to his will, not those around him. When we submit to God's will and purpose, we are likewise empowered for the job.

Again, self-caring is not the same as being self-centered. A self-caring woman will not abandon her faith in order to keep a partner or anyone else happy. She will be able to say "no" to any behavior or activity that is not in line with her God-centered knowledge. We aren't asked by God to be pious, but I believe we are asked to have clear boundaries and do what it takes to protect our spirits from harm.

CONGRUENCY FOR THE UMPTEENTH TIME

Congruency becomes even more vital for the woman of faith. Not only does her own inner knowledge and her behavior have to match up, but in addition, these things also have to line up with what God says. Since the *knowing* part of me believes that his words of instruction are in my best interest, I am congruent when *being* what I *know*. I am certainly a far cry from complete; I will always be a work in progress. Women of faith look not only inward, but upward, seeking to be true not only to themselves, but wanting to be true to their maker.

WHERE DO I BEGIN?
Taking the Responsibility...Again

Some of us may start out blaming our partner when we finally recognize our spiritually starved state; "I stopped going to church because he wouldn't go with me." However, as we mature, we realize that our current state is really all about us, our choices, our lack of assertiveness, and our lack of congruency. More women at midlife are taking responsibility for feeding their neglected spirits. Just as it is in our relationships with men, it is only when we accept full responsibility for our choices that we can be empowered to do something about our relationship with God.

Many of the women I see in therapy reveal that they once had a strong faith but neglected this belief during their early adult years because of disapproval from a boyfriend or spouse. I am one of those women who, for several years after falling in love, neglected her spirit and ignored her faith. I allowed fear of my partner's disapproval to make me incongruent. But fortunately, an incongruent state causes discomfort, and internal discomfort motivates us to seek change.

Humility, Receptivity, and Change

If you feel a longing to renew your faith or to begin a new journey of faith, start with humility, receptivity, and repentance. You might say to me, but you have been talking about confidence and empowerment; why are you telling me to be humble? I believe to access God's power, we must first acknowledge the limits of our own knowledge and power. A humble heart is receptive to a new spirit and a new way of looking at things; an arrogant spirit is not. Opening up your heart is the first step on a faith journey.

The next step takes you to the written source for me of instruction and inspiration. The Bible, God's message to us earthlings, advises us how best to live our lives. As a Christian, I would first recommend reading the gospel of John, which is the fourth book of the New Testament. The book of John contains the essence of Christ's message and much of the needed information for the person who is new or returning to her faith.

The third step, which requires humility, concerns repentance. Repentance is, of course, more than sorrow for wrongdoing; it involves change. I don't want to say I'm sorry and then keep doing the same things. True repentance involves turning from our old ways and searching out God's plan.

Get Support

There is no last step, as living in faith is an ongoing process that doesn't end until we die. Getting involved with other people who share your faith is very important. Isolation enables separation and doubt, just as it does in our earthly relationships. It's not that God is going to abandon us if we don't have other believers around, but we are more likely to be weak and *abandon him* if we lack the support of other believers. It is also a good idea to become part of a smaller study or growth group if you are just beginning or renewing your commitments. In small groups it is easier to form relationships and feel part of a church family.

But There Are a Lot of Hypocrites Out There...

As you strive for maturity, you'll realize that your church or place of worship is made up of ordinary people like you and me, and it is therefore flawed. Don't be quick to throw up your hands and walk away when you see problems there. If you go to church and look to your fellow worshippers as shining examples, you're sure to be disappointed. People with greed, pride, or control issues are there hopefully recognizing their flaws and looking for divine help in overcoming them. Maybe God isn't finished working on them yet, and your patience and acceptance can only help them.

Don't go to a place of worship just to get something, but go to give something. If I go just to *get,* then I always come away a bit disappointed. By giving heartfelt worship, whether through song, prayer, money offering, or service, I will *experience* church rather than just *attend* church.

DON'T BEGIN THE JOURNEY WITHOUT FUELING UP

What a difference a few minutes can make. Beginning a new day's journey without food for my spirit can leave me running on empty and possibly unable to make difficult choices. When we lack physical energy (because we're hungry) we just can't push ourselves when the going gets tough. If I'm serious about finding my real passion and purpose in life, I can't afford to miss my connections due to a sluggish spirit. A daily devotional, with time for meditation and prayer, needs to become part of your routine if you are looking to keep your spirit strong.

Using a Daily Devotional Book

I also like to read from a daily devotional book. A girlfriend gave me one entitled *God Calling,* which contains a short, inspirational reading for each day. I am amazed at what comes to my spirit through these short passages. The two women who let God inspire them to write this book remain anonymous, calling themselves "two listeners." I had many interruptions when trying to write this chapter, and I felt less than encouraged about my ability to write something so important. Then I read a passage from *God Calling*. It said: "Shut out the distractions of the world...Meditate on all I say. Ponder it. Not to draw your own conclusions, but to absorb Mine." I was quickly calmed, reassured, and redirected.

Listen

If in my devotional time I only read and pray, but allow no time of silent meditation, then there is no time for my spirit to *listen.* I need still time in order for that small voice to be heard by my spirit. During this quiet time the words that I read can speak to me, and my thoughts are free to be directed. Clearing our minds of shopping lists, daily duties, and general worries is the only way that we can be on the receiving end if we want to hear from God. I believe in those still moments, God can take the words that I read and, in my heart and mind, apply it to me. Use some quiet time for meditating and listening.

And remember, a quiet time can not only happen during a planned morning devotional, it can be any moment that you intentionally focus on God—you might just be watering the flowers or peeling the potatoes!

USING YOUR FAITH IN FINDING YOUR PURPOSE

Your Main Purpose is Outlined in Your "Owners Manual"

Now that you have emptied yourself of the negative or conflicting outside voices that drove your actions, you are able to hear and experience your own heart's longings. I believe that because God created us, he has placed within each of us a longing for a connection with his spirit. When we invite God into our lives, he can work through our hands, our voice, and our hearts and minds, no matter how humanly weak our "self" is. God's purpose for channeling his sprit through us is so that it can flow into the lives of others. Our job is simply not to block the flow, but to willingly open our hearts and minds to it. If I do that, good things will flow through me whether I am a secretary, bank executive, attorney, doctor, or factory worker.

Our Purpose is Progress

My daily devotional book says, "Progress is the Law of Heaven." It goes on to explain that our goal should be to rise a little higher each day—become more knowledgeable, more loving, more brave, and more strong. In other words, the very *purpose* of our lives is to make *progress* in every area of our lives. My prayer each day is to be a better mother, wife, therapist, friend, sister, and neighbor than I was yesterday. Each day I strive to be a little less selfish, whiney or lazy, and maybe just to be a little more thoughtful of people who are less fortunate than I am.

Is There Just One Choice for Each Person?

Does God have just this one thing, one job, planned for me? Is there just one purpose for each person, and, if I miss it, is it then too late? Well, it is my belief that God's purpose is to love and please him, and we can do that in many different areas of work or areas of interest.

Thankfully, he does present more than one opportunity to us in life. If you're not living a congruent life and miss this opportunity, you can recommit your life and then be in the right place spiritually to seize the next opportunity. You can miss an opportunity if you happen to be off track due to fear, anger, a bad relationship, or because you are listening to others instead of your God-given knowledge.

I personally believe that we don't always find our passion or purpose through our employment. Some people work at a job in order to have money to engage in something they feel passionately about. If I am doing activities that I feel excited about on weekends or evenings, it might even affect my attitude and usefulness on my nine to five job. In the meantime, I can be a beacon of light, even in a boring office job, if I'm feeding my passion when I'm at home. I believe having the right spirit, even in the "wrong" job, can lead to a more meaningful and purposeful life.

Finding Meaning and Purpose Where You Are

Women of faith can trust that God will use them wherever and in whatever situation they find themselves. You may not feel that you have found your life's "dream" yet, but today, at the office, you might allow yourself to comfort or encourage someone who is struggling. Today you may not be clear on a topic that you are passionate about, but your kindness to someone who is feeling hopeless may make a difference in their desire to live or die. If you get too caught up in following a "dream" or searching "out there" for a special purpose, then you could miss daily opportunities to bring significance and joy to your life today.

Many women find purpose in creating a good home and a safe, loving environment for their children. What could have more value than preparing and equipping children for life in a harsh world? We're not all led down the same path, but we'll never know what God's opinion is if we don't seek it out.

BUT I'M NOT WELL EQUIPPED
Increased Courage Through Increased Reliance

In the spiritual world it's okay to be dependent. In the human world we are bound to be disappointed if we depend on others for our direction and our happiness. God knows who I really am and the direction I should take, so reliance on him is always in my best interest and will always increase my confidence.

"Fear Not"

Fear paralyzes. Are you allowing your personal fears to hinder you from being what God wants you to be, or to have what he wants you to have? If you think of yourself as "less than," you probably doubt God's interest in you. God didn't create you to be "less than;" he envisioned you meeting the potential that he gave you. He sees the best in you and is willing to forgive all the mistakes or bad things you have done. God doesn't want us living in fear.

We need courage to take a stand against what we know is not right; we are surrounded today by a lack of integrity, compromise, and slack morals. Taking the higher road to do what we know is right makes it more likely that other people will do the same. Set an example of integrity. Don't follow the crowd; lead, and the crowd just might follow you.

Faith is Not a Feeling

Faith in God is difficult for many people because they can't prove God's existence. I now realize that faith is a choice. Having faith is a conscious choice for some individuals as opposed to a natural capability. Another concept that I have learned is that faith is not a feeling; when things don't "feel" so good, my faith continues by *choice*. Even people who were raised in a particular faith must come to an adult decision regarding their earlier teachings or beliefs. Most of my women friends have made faith in God their choice and see the need to incorporate that faith into their daily lives.

Flawed Like Me

In examining some of the characters in the Bible who did great things, I discovered that most of them had major flaws and had made serious mistakes in their lives.

So many people believe that the Bible is not relevant for them because they relate it to saints and very pious people who did great things. First of all, we have to remember that Jesus chose ordinary people—fishermen and tent makers—for his inner circle; he did not surround himself with intellectuals, pious leaders of the faith community, or the rich and famous.

We don't have to be good enough to do historic things, but we have to have faith and a willingness to do important things. We are all flawed, but we can be used in spite of our flaws. I saw a marquee in front of a church the other day that read:"God doesn't just choose the equipped, he equips the chosen." Quit thinking you're not good enough;

you simply have to be *willing* and have faith. Take responsibility for getting yourself spiritually equipped, and know that this "equipment" is available to everybody who asks.

QUESTIONS AND SUGGESTIONS

Question: If you have neglected your spirit due to fear of damaging the stability of your relationship, or efforts to keep someone else happy, do you now find yourself fearful of beginning a faith journey?
Suggestion: Start by finding your owner's manual. If your Bible is missing, shop for one that you like. The King James Version uses old English, so you might search for something like the New International Version, which uses more modern language. Shop for a daily devotional, too; there are devotionals and studies written just for women.

Question: What is your current spiritual status? On a scale from one to ten, with "one" meaning "totally neglected" and "ten" meaning "daily priority," how attentive have you been to your spirit?
Suggestion: If you rated yourself a "five" or less, write down the behaviors that show you are taking back responsibility for your own spiritual state. For instance, you might be reinstituting a daily devotional into your schedule, attending a weekly worship service, or joining a women's Bible study.

Question: Do you have a scheduled time each day when you can be alone in a quiet place for reading, prayer, and meditation?
Suggestion: Find out what is best for you by committing to a one-week trial for the time you think is going to work best. If you are generally too sleepy by the time you get household chores done in the evening, then start out with a morning time. Like physical exercise, if it's not in the schedule, it won't happen.

9 Sex, Lies, and the Midlife Marriage

As a woman's focus moves more toward a rediscovery of her true self, increased energy will be spent gaining emotional independence and personal fulfillment. She may ask herself important questions: Can she possibly navigate these personal changes without compromising her marriage? How does a woman become more true to her self, search for her own purpose and meaning, and reach out to women friends while remaining committed to her marriage? And how can she know what mature love is supposed to encompass.

THE HIDDEN TRUTH

Many women are afraid to tell each other about their real feelings on the subject of sex and marriage. Outside of the therapy office or my close circle of friends, I'm more likely to get mere hints as to the real attitudes that women have. But if you are tuned in to these "hints," you can still get the picture. The eye rolls, the side comments, and even the jokes give a clue to the real attitudes held by many women. The women that don't know me very well, and even some who do, back up when it comes to sharing feelings, attitudes, and experiences related to sex and marriage. However, I believe that they are more concerned with their image than with bashfulness about these intimate topics.

Concerns about the effects of gossip are legitimate and may prevent open sharing about sex and marriage. I have observed too that many women try to protect their husbands' images and therefore may give no more than hints about the real states of their intimate relationships and behaviors in the marriage. I'm not implying that this tendency is necessarily a bad thing, but I am saying that it makes it very hard to get an accurate read on how things really are in the average midlife marriage.

It is my belief that the baby boomer generation will get increasingly open about the realities of this stage of life. Yet, I have to interject here that a midlife woman's attitude can be as varied as her life situation. She may have been married to the same person over twenty years, she may be divorced and not dating, she may be single and dating, or she may have just married or remarried. We can't lump these women together as they vary mentally, emotionally, and situationally. I have a great deal of professional and personal experience with women that are in long-term marriages, whether it is their first, second, or third marriages. Most of my friends are in marriages that have endured the long haul, and even those in second marriages have been in them for more than ten years.

Women are much more likely to talk about intimate areas of life than men are, even when they hardly know you. At one social gathering at a friend's house I was talking with several women that I had never met before, but who were long time friends of my friend. I can't say exactly how the topic came up, but soon we were discussing our lack of sex drive, and several of the women agreed that if their husbands didn't initiate sex, that it would probably never happen. One shared her fantasy of having her own room where she could lie in bed, watch television, and actually keep it on one station for the entire length of a show. Another said that she would just like to be able to turn the television off when she felt like going to sleep.

FANTASY VERSUS REALITY IN THE LONGTERM MARRIAGE
The Hollywood Version

On one television interview I watched a glamorous midlife movie star talk about sex being so much more wonderful now that she was fifty. She, of course, looked like a million dollars as she laughed and referred to her partner, who is also a gorgeous movie star. If I didn't have so many women friends and so many women clients, I might really feel inadequate. The movies often portray mature women as having huge sexual appetites, but my experience tells me something very different. Most of the mature women to whom I talk have decreased interests in sex, or almost no sex drive; some admit to a mere tolerance for sex in their marriages.

Although most midlife women are not changing themselves to match Hollywood's fantasy woman, some are running to the nearest plastic surgeon. On the other hand, many are working hard to improve their inner selves. While I believe there's certainly nothing wrong with getting a tuck here and there if it makes you feel better or more able to compete in our youth-oriented work world, some women become obsessed with their wrinkles while failing to notice their needs for internal makeovers.

Much to my husband's horror, I will openly share here that sex is near the bottom of my priority list at this particular time in my life. It is to his horror that I say it out loud, and it is to his horror that it is the gospel truth. I also think that many midlife men don't have greater drives than women, but due to their increased insecurity at midlife they are more apt to look to sex as a means to feel loved and secure with their partners.

The Ideal Marriage

The ideal midlife relationship is one in which there are two individuals who are independent, yet joined together, working sometimes in different directions while supporting and nurturing each other. They are secure enough in themselves so they are comfortable with distance as well as closeness. It isn't about submission and domination; it isn't about ownership or competition. In other sections of Anne Morrow Lindbergh's book, *Gift From The Sea,* she uses the oyster shell as a metaphor for the marriage relationship. She describes it as awkward and ugly, slate-colored and unsymmetrical, not beautiful but functional, comfortable and familiar. Yet she doesn't want to put it down or leave it. She also sees a positive to middle age as a "second flowering, second growth, even a kind of second adolescence"..."tragically misunderstood by society who may view it as a period of decline." She sees the midlife years of marriage as having great potential if each partner reaches beyond the marriage in order to expand and develop themselves.

THE REALITY OF THE MIDLIFE MARRIAGE

Opposites Attract

We've all heard the saying "opposites attract," and this view holds a lot of weight when it comes to understanding marriages and what happens over time. Opposites attract alright; in the beginning this factor is so exciting and romantic that it causes sparks to fly. We are drawn to "difference" like a magnet, yet we can convince ourselves that there is so much in common. Almost every couple I can think of is composed of opposite personality types. How many extroverts do you know married introverts? How many "neatnicks" do you know married slobs? It's almost as if we search out that quality that we lack and try to get it through marriage. Or do we search out that quality we don't like and then try to fix it? Harville Hendrix in his book, *Getting the Love You Want,* theorizes that we seek partners with the same negative quality that one of our caretakers had (the one that frustrated our love needs) and then try to work the lack out in our marriages. We try to feel love by the new person with that quality; we're attracted to what's familiar, even if it is negative.

My union had a very romantic beginning. My husband is a Pollyanna optimist and I am a die-hard realist. My husband has an "it's only money" attitude, and I have a "oh, my heavens, we'll go broke" attitude. My husband goes and never stops, and I can't cope without downtime and plenty of rest. My husband can give a speech on the spur of the moment on any topic to an audience of seven thousand, while I must plan for three weeks for a short talk to an audience of twenty.

The funny thing is although most people are attracted to opposites, they will then spend the next thirty years trying to change their partners and make them more like themselves. Many spouses will also be angry for most of those years because our partners aren't cooperating with our generous and thoughtful efforts to change them. When I counsel couples for marital therapy, I usually ask them to tell me what attracted them to each other. It's almost comical how the very things that they found attractive in the beginning are the things that drive them crazy now. The problem is that over time differences wear on us, and we start to build up resentment about those little things that daily get on our nerves. We may even become contemptuous toward our spouse, which, according to research done by psychologist John Gottman, is a predictor of failure for the marriage.

We take these things personally now, as if our partner's personality quirks are there just to annoy us. We accepted those quirks as charming in the romantic phase of the relationships, but we often view them as personal attacks on our pursuit of happiness as the years wear on. If we are building up anger and resentment, it affects every interaction we have with our partners, and before long the relationships can be tainted with hostility. It's one thing to have "moments" of hostility, but when it seeps into every other thing we do or say to each other, then these relationships will start to sour.

In John Gottman's book, *Why Marriages Succeed or Fail,* he observed that marriages can have nasty interactions without dooming the marriage if there are five positive interactions for each negative or hostile one. According to his long term research, even a volatile couple can be successful if the five-to-one ratio is met. After my husband and I did a marriage workshop for a church group a few years ago, the participants presented us with a plaque that read, "Marriage is made in heaven… but then so is thunder and lightning."

Why do so few couples come close to the ideal state of marriage after midlife? Were marriages doing better, say, in the 1950s? Fifty years ago life moved at a less hectic pace. The energy that it took to maintain day-to-day relationships was therefore more available. Yet some women likely stayed in marriages simply for financial security, as many job markets weren't yet open to them. There was certainly a lack of equality and women lacked the choices available to men. While there was more time and energy for relationships, there wasn't the freedom for personal growth and expansion. When I reflect on my parents and their friends relationships, I can't remember one marriage that I can truly say was anywhere near "ideal." The only ideal marriages that I recall were on television shows like "Leave it to Beaver," "I love Lucy," or "The Donna Reed Show."

The Dependency Flip-Flop

Marriages can turn upside down after a midlife crisis and the changes that follow. Those that survive the upheaval will settle down, but the marriage won't look the same as it did before. The balance of power between the two people has likely shifted. Many midlife marriages will experience a total flip-flop as there are changes in personal direction, career positions, social connections, and parenting demands.

Men who may have been in a career since their twenties may now be threatened by younger men training to be their replacement. They may also have to cut back hours due to health concerns, approaching retirement, or, being the higher-paid employees, they may be threatened with a forced, early retirement. Many women in their fifties, however, may be approaching their height of success since they got a later start, or are now giving their careers more focus with the kids out of the house.

When women in midlife begin to change and grow in new directions, men may become more insecure. One of the known differences in men and women is that men feel loved if they are getting sex, while women must feel loved to even want sex (assuming there is a sex drive present). If sex is what makes men feel more secure and loved, you can see why they might feel insecure when women lose interest in sex as they branch out in their social lives or careers.

Men at midlife may have few friends, and may rely on their wives alone for friendship. I recently counseled a man in my office who, at age fifty four, was having problems at his job that could have jeopardized his career, retirement, and reputation in the community. He was naturally distraught, but his typical coping strategy—sharing with his wife and allowing her to carry some of the burden—wasn't working this time. "She's my only friend, and I count on her when things go wrong," he lamented. It turned out his wife was having health problems and stress with her own job, and was in no position to be leaned on. This reliance on wives alone as confidantes and best friends can cause a shakeup in the marriage as women in their fifties come into their own, discover things they are passionate about, find more friends, and expand their interest away from the home. They may have been more dependent on their husbands in the first ten or fifteen years of marriage, but the last ten or fifteen years may see a reverse with wives having the stronger sense of independence. Husbands may now be more emotionally dependent on wives, but it can be a hostile dependency, as they may be quite uncomfortable in dependent roles.

Change Can be Threatening

Obviously, couples where men are less emotionally dependent will do best during this stage of life. The few who have strong male support groups will have the smoothest transition into the midlife marriage. If your husband confides in you alone about his feelings of insecurity, it might change what you do for yourself and you might stall in your own efforts to blossom and grow. If you revert back to your earlier ways just to keep him from feeling threatened, the marriage might survive, but you may feel that you're being held back.

To further complicate the middle-years marriage, a man may be feeling a pull toward home and family relationships just as his wife is starting her pull away from the home front. The hard-working husband in his forties or fifties may be realizing what he has missed or neglected and may now be ready to slow down and give his wife more time and attention. He may be weary of sixty-hour work weeks and even a little guilty about his inattentiveness at home.

But just as this shift begins for him, his wife is discovering her abilities and opportunities for interests outside the home. If the husband can overcome his anxiety about these changes in his wife and support and encourage her search, the marriage can flourish. However, he must be willing to connect with her on a different level than he did years ago.

Balancing Endless Choices

Women now have career choices that they lacked in the past, yet they are stressed most of the time and their marriages often take the brunt of that stress. In a society where we try to do it all—give our kids everything, expand our personal growth, take care of aging parents, and head three committees at church—we just might come up a tad short on energy for our spouses. As the pendulum has swung from oppression toward freedom for women, the change has left couples off balance and whirling with confusion. If you locked a group of people outside a candy store for years, allowing them to only look in the window, what would happen if you unlocked the door one day? They would probably eat with a vengeance, perhaps to the point of making themselves ill.

That's how I view women as the doors of opportunity to work in what had been strictly a "man's world" were finally unlocked. We understandably ran in and grabbed all we could. The *choice* part of this new deal soon became overlooked, and women sometimes went to work outside the home feeling it was expected of them. Many households quickly became dependent on the dual income, and thus the real lack of "choice."

At about the same time, the pendulum was swinging from punitive and restrictive to indulgent and permissive with regards to children. We couldn't give our children enough toys, high-tech electronic gadgets, dance lessons, music lessons, or sports training. We tolerated behaviors that our parents would have never tolerated; we became too accepting of unacceptable behavior. Misbehaving kids add to our stress.

Now that mom is working eight to five, and the kids have soccer, piano lessons, and drama camp, dad has decided to open his own small business since he has the security of mom's income as backup. There is often no formal supper because nobody has time to cook it. The house doesn't settle down from all the running around until well after eight or nine at night because the kids are not home until then. You have a couple of loads of laundry to do and you have to be in bed by ten o' clock in order to get up at six and start all over again. Do you really feel like having sex when you have barely spoken to your husband, and when you did, it was an irritable exchange about who was going to take the dog out?

There is a major lack of common sense in the way we live today. The way we hustle and bustle about in our chaotic lifestyle has a huge effect on the quality of our marriages. In order to improve the state of marriage in America, we must come back to a common sense approach to work, running the home, and managing our children. I do realize that this "chaos" is an extreme reaction and a natural initial response to the many new choices and changes taking place in our society. However, I do think it's time that we begin to move toward a more moderate and balanced lifestyle, lest we do ourselves in. In couple's therapy I refer to the pyramid – the couple is at the top, and if they are doing well, it trickles down to the kids. If the couple relationship is nurtured and healthy, the kids feel secure and free to venture out and explore in safety.

Our fairy tale version of what wedlock should be, our chaotic lifestyles, and our irrational need to let children have and do it all contribute to the state of today's marriage. I don't have all of the answers for creating that perfect balance, but surely we could make a few common sense changes to start the pendulum moving back toward center. Women need to remember that work outside the home is a choice; making it a necessity defeats the purpose. A home really doesn't run itself; it needs a good and present manager.

The man sometimes may actually be more suited (by personality or profession) to stay home or work part-time in order to take care of the home and the kids. Children really don't need so many organized activities and they surely won't die if they can't do everything they ask to do. If we believe our children must be happy at all times, we are setting them up to have unrealistic expectations, and therefore sure disappointment. The decisions about managing the home require common sense; they need to be made in a realistic way so as to create balance, not a ridiculous hectic schedule. We can only be good marriage partners and parents if we are not perpetually exhausted.

AN AFFAIR—THE SHOW STOPPER
Personal Growth Delayed

The dependency flip-flop is true of many midlife marriages, but mainly for those that survived without anyone having an affair. In a marriage where the forty to fifty-something man had an affair but stayed with the wife, she may now feel unable to proceed to the next stage of her own personal growth as she regresses to focus on her husband and how she can hold on to him. When the rug is pulled out from under a marriage by an affair, it halts a woman's normal progression toward personal growth and independence.

It has been my observation that marriages are less likely to survive when the woman is the one who has the affair. Women seem to have affairs due to true unhappiness with marriages and their marriage partners, where men seem to be more able to compartmentalize their lives, mentally separating affairs from their marriages, even when their marriages are good. I remember in graduate school reading about research that showed women were more likely to leave marriages because they were truly unhappy, whereas men would leave marriages only after they had found other partners. Even though the numbers are changing as women's lives become more parallel to men's in the workplace, men are still more likely to have an extramarital affair. Therefore, if a man is caught in an affair while in what seems an adequate marriage, the wife is more likely to jump in and try to fix it. The woman is less likely to step out in the first place if she deemed the marriage as adequate.

THE NEGLECTED ROLE OF ACCEPTANCE IN MARRIAGE
Accepting That Marriage Can't Totally Fulfill Me

There are many kinds of marriages out there, and therefore few generalizations can be made. Too many, however, are what I call "the committed, but not ecstatically happy." This is not something that is talked about frequently or openly. I am referring to the couple in their forties or fifties who, through the years of change, wind up not liking each other very much. They don't hate each other; in fact, they might love each other as one loves family…they just don't *like* each other. This can occur when we refuse to accept what can't be changed in our partners, such as personality traits or basic beliefs.

Midlife women in therapy often express this unsettling feeling of dislike for their partners, yet come to a conclusion that they will never leave the marriage. After weighing the consequences of ending a twenty-five-year marriage, they decide that the possible damage would be too much for themselves and their families. These women have pleaded with their husbands to come into therapy or to make certain changes, all to no avail. Even if these women open themselves up to women friends, new experiences, and new directions, there remains a gap that they erroneously believe is preventing them from being "whole" or "complete."

Many women in long-term marriages are realizing that although it would be nice to feel successful in all areas of life, they may need to accept partial completeness. Some women in midlife marriages, whose husbands show an unwillingness to expand and change, will decide to stay and focus their energies in other directions. They have decided that the devastation of divorce is worse than the gap caused by a "blah" marriage. From my vantage point, this type of marriage is the most common, with great marital partnerships on one end of the bell-shaped curve and those "disaster" relationships on the other end.

Even though a partner can't change his or her personality traits, there may still be adequate points of common interest where the couple can connect if attitudes aren't too hostile. Doing simple activities together, such as yard work, cooking, interacting with children, or enjoying friends, can provide moments of connection and positive interaction. Couples whose positive interactions outweigh the negative, and those who accept and show respect for one another, can still survive. So the midlife woman who has focused on personal growth, pursued her own dreams,and has women friends can, with these moments of connection, find herself with an adequate level of completeness.

Accepting My Partner's Flaws and Differences

Some observations that I have made regarding long-term marriages of couples approaching their fifties are: Those who make them work have been able to do the following: (1) They have let go of grudges, hurts, and disappointments from the past. The last stage of grief is *acceptance*, and past losses and disappointments must be successfully forgiven. I personally believe that ninety-nine percent of us go through a sort of grieving in a long-term marriage. Even if we didn't buy fully into the fairy tale, we all find that our dream, or some part of our dream about what marriage was supposed to be like, gets busted. Lost dreams are grieved. Couples that get stuck in the past, or grieving lost dreams, can't grow and change as needed through life transitions. (2) They have matured in their ability to accept their partner's flaws and certain personality traits and beliefs. After some seventeen years of marriage, you accept that your husband is never going to think of flowers for "no reason" or surprise you with a candlelight dinner, as he is just not a spontaneous, romantic kind of guy. You have the choice of *accepting* his personality or being mad at him for the next one hundred years! (3) They have matured in their knowledge and ability to not make other people's stuff about them. In other words, the little piles that my husband creates all over the house are not about me, but about him and his personality. I spent years taking them very personally, certain that he was being passive- aggressive, or just bent on driving me crazy. Now I don't even bother to wonder *why*, but figure that whatever it is, it's about him and who he is, not about me. (4) They have the maturity to know that love is a choice, not just a feeling. Just like faith is not a feeling, but a choice, love must be something that you decide on. Once the romantic stage has passed, your actions create the feelings, where before it was your feelings that created the actions. Now those actions are intentional, purposeful, and the result of a clear decision on your part. You can choose to act in a way that creates communication and love.

There's much more that needs to be said about "acceptance." Most marriage therapy focuses on the need to *change*; few deal with the need to *accept*. We come or bring our partners into therapy with the goal of changing; in fact, therapy is deemed a failure or a success based on someone's "change." To be successfully married, we need to accept that most personality traits (not transient behaviors) and core beliefs of our partners probably won't change that much. That means also that some conflicts are not resolvable. My husband is never going to "slow down" no matter how much I tell him he's going to make himself physically ill. Couples have to agree to disagree on some things and respect their partners' needs to think or do it differently.

Women also need to accept that their husbands can't be their girlfriends. With all of the changes that have taken place in the roles of men and women over the last couple of decades, men are more confused than ever about what women want and expect from them. If you're looking for your husband to be your girlfriend, you have set him up for sure failure.

Accepting That Marriage is a Series of Peaks and Valleys

Our feelings come from the beliefs and meanings that we put on things. If I believe being irritated and aggravated with my husband means that our marriage is a mistake, then that belief will affect how I feel; that, in turn, will affect how I act. But if I believe that these valleys (and peaks) are a normal part of a long-term relationship, I will feel better about my marriage and act accordingly.

Most women in midlife have accepted that there will be regular intervals when they are very angry at their husbands, when things feel distant and out of sorts. When I was younger I put an ominous meaning on these uncomfortable spells and thoughts. Now I know that they will pass. Unless there has been a major break in trust, a woman can experience this kind of tension, and yet feel confident that "this too will pass." Peaks and valleys exist even if you're married to Mr. Right.

THINGS I WILL NOT ACCEPT

Clear Individual Boundaries

Marriages that have clear boundaries are more likely to survive the long haul. There are personal boundaries held by each individual, as well as couple boundaries enforced by the partnership. When I describe personal boundaries to clients, I ask them to imagine themselves standing in the center of a circle. The circle represents a boundary and everything inside the circle is the stuff in life that is clearly in their best interest, while the stuff outside the circle is clearly not good for them. It is their job, their responsibility, in life to let good things into the circle and to keep the bad stuff out. Too many women let other people decide for them what goes in or out of the circle.

I have my own clear boundaries and won't accept lying, deception, or "secrets." I won't accept infidelity; it's clearly not in my best interest. I won't accept verbal or physical abuse. Yes, I know that there are midlife women living in abusive relationships; fortunately, many are recognizing their responsibility to enforce the boundaries of their own lives. If women look to men to take care of them and decide what is good for them, they are vulnerable to victimization. To the media's credit, there are now many talk shows, documentaries, and news features that have made women more aware of these issues.

I won't accept addiction inside the circle; it's never in my best interest. Addiction isn't always about drugs or alcohol. Addiction to pornography is on the rise, and I see women struggling to squeeze this into the circle in order to keep their marriages intact. They believe that pornography is a bad thing and that addiction is a bad thing, yet they have let those addictions in because, "*He said* it's not hurting anybody." I've seen young women with husbands who are addicted to exercise, allowing running and weightlifting to take priority in their lives. Many of these women are profoundly disappointed, lonely, and lack security in their marriage relationships. In their cases, exercise has become something more than a way to stay fit and healthy.

Ring Around The Couple – Couple Boundaries

The couple, like the individual, has an invisible circle around it, and it is the couple's job to keep out all that works against their best interests. This can be tricky when, at the same time, each partner may be expanding his or her reach outside the circle to include new friends, new ideas, and new experiences. Friends can become a threat to the marriage if they become first priority to the exclusion of the partner's needs and feelings. Women must handle the demands of friends and groups with maturity. They need to support each other's need to be there when families need them, while also supporting the necessity of getting together when they can. It always comes down to that simple word, *balance*.

Entanglement With Grown Children

Adult children can become a challenge to the midlife couple's boundaries. As individuals, and as a partnership unit, we must agree to take responsibility for setting limits when the marriage is being negatively affected. We may have to face that our own individual behavior is creating conflict, or that our joint pattern of dealing with adult children is keeping us from working on our own life tasks or pursuing our joint dreams.

Lynn, a fifty-three-year-old woman I counseled, seemed depressed as she admitted to conflict in her second marriage of twelve years. She had grown children from another marriage who became involved with drugs and were always in a mess. She was caught up in a "rescuing" behavior and was in the habit of giving them money when they were in a jam. Her frustrated husband refused to let her children visit their home and, therefore, a major conflict developed in the marriage. He could not trust her to set boundaries with her grown children, so he tried to keep them away.

It can be a vicious cycle if the marriage is conflicted due to over involvement with grown kids. Partners failing to set boundaries with adult children may get even more involved with them as a way of keeping the focus off of a bad marriage. If the focus stays on the kids, the marriage may look okay on the surface, but the only thing keeping them going is their need to "fix" their flailing adult children. The sad part is that these dysfunctional grown children are kept dysfunctional by this co-dependent relationship with parents. I've also seen midlife couples where one or both get so involved with the grandkids that it takes the focus off of their miserable marital relationship. These scenarios generally occur when there has not been that burst of personal growth or branching out for each partner, and the individuals feel stuck. Individual satisfaction increases the likelihood of couple satisfaction; those who take responsibility for their individual happiness are more likely to find couple happiness. If men knew this, they would be less threatened by women seeking individual satisfaction, significance, and purpose.

WHEN ALL ELSE FAILS—THE MIDLIFE DIVORCE
Surviving the Loss

As a young therapist, I used to be bent on saving marriages, even bad ones. In my middle years I have made a change and am more able to recognize when someone needs to give up the effort and try to find personal happiness. If a marriage is so uncomfortable that it zaps a woman's emotional energy, and she has given it her best for years, I fully support a decision to leave the marriage. A bad marriage that never gets significantly better will drain and preoccupy a woman, preventing her from pursuing her own purpose and passion in life. Few of us are strong enough to emotionally separate ourselves from a bad marriage and still remain whole, going on and succeeding on a personal level.

It is my opinion that midlife can be the most difficult age for women to divorce. At this point many women in long-term marriages are unprepared to financially support themselves (especially if they have put careers on hold for children) and many have neither the experience nor skills to re-enter the work force at an advanced level. Again, on the bell-shaped curve, there is the one end where the couple has enough assets to divide, leaving the woman financially secure; on the other end of the curve the woman ends up destitute. In the center of the curve lies the majority, where the woman will survive, but will lose her sense of financial security and will probably have to accept a change in lifestyle. And her dreams for retirement, and the retirement lifestyle that she wanted, are shaken.

Women in their thirties who are going through divorce are usually eligible for child support if minor children are involved and sometimes alimony and, although fearful, they are young enough to move into the workforce with time to progress to higher levels. Younger women, no matter how apprehensive about surviving without husbands, are still nowhere as vulnerable as women over fifty, who may be lacking the education or training to compete in today's job market. These older women are also worried about age discrimination, as well as possible health issues.

One friend, age fifty and recently divorced, told me that it was hard for her to face the reality that in addition to losing her children at this stage of life (they are off to college), she was losing her partner. Her dreams of retirement had not been for "a party of one." She said, "My lowest time came when I was hit with the reality of being a family of one when I had been a family of four. The upside was that I had to re-evaluate my life out of necessity. The old ways in which she viewed herself, the old ways she managed her social life (through his business friends), and her old pattern of self-sufficiency no longer worked. Without family in the area, she was forced to rely on friends. She admits that in the past she has kept others at a distance but, "now I couldn't build a shell thick enough." She went on to laugh about the house repairs she has learned to do, and says that she is more confident about everything except… money. It's the same story I have heard many times. Many midlife women are able to gain the confidence needed to manage after divorce; it's the money issues that plague them the most.

Though it is not an admitted viewpoint, I believe some men are motivated to keep power over women for fear that if women had equal money they would not stay with them when they misbehave. That brings us back to the old idea that men need to feel power over women in order to "have" them. In cave man days, muscles and a big club did the trick; in Biblical times owning land and cattle gave men power; in modern times, being able to earn more money in the workplace gives men power.

Letting Go When it is in Your Best Interest

Women who have stayed in bad marriages for many years and have therefore been unable to focus on themselves and experience personal growth spurts will be more devastated if their relationships end at midlife. These women lack adequate emotional growth and will most likely avoid divorce if at all possible; they are the women who are apt to stay with cheating husbands or alcoholics.

Two of my women clients have both been in thirty-year marriages. Both told stories about their husbands' repeated affairs and, to top it off, both husbands had produced babies from their affairs. These men stayed involved with their girlfriends and children they had fathered. One woman, who was in her late fifties, told how her husband, even now, continues to flirt with other women in her presence, embarrassing her and making her feel inadequate. She had for years excused his bad behavior, feeling it was about her; she allowed him to make her feel badly about herself. Her resentment had built up over the years, and instead of taking responsibility for her own happiness by leaving him and moving on, she stayed to punish him. I pointed out to her that she was sacrificing her one and only life in order to stick it to her husband, who was having a good old time.

My other client was in her forties and on disability due to ill health. Her entire life revolved around her husband and his many affairs. She regularly called people at his place of employment to get the name of his latest fling. She confronted some of these women and regularly followed up on leads that she got from finding papers with phone numbers and women's names in his pants pockets. She never left, and she convinced herself that it was because she loved him; after all, *he said* he loved her. The crisis that precipitated her visit to a therapist was that her husband suddenly left her.

She was hysterical for several days before a relative convinced her to see a counselor. As with her life, she spent much of her therapy time focused on her husband and was unable to use her time and money to work on herself. No matter how hard I pressed, she was unwilling to focus on her own life, her fears, her strengths, and her very own dreams. Unfortunately, both of these women had become so entrenched in their own patterns of focusing outwardly instead of inwardly, that neither was able to let go and act in their own best interests.

"I Wish I Would Have Gotten Out Twenty Years Ago"

Many women in midlife going through divorce would advise younger women not to wait twenty years to see if partners continue chronic patterns of destructive behavior. Do what is reasonable to request and support change on his part, but if it doesn't happen, don't put your life on hold indefinitely while hanging on to false hopes. Look at the evidence, not the feelings, and get professional help if you see yourself paralyzed with fear.

There is much more to say about midlife divorce. For now, I just want to emphasize the point that although divorce is not a good thing, it is sometimes the lesser of two evils. I would tell younger women that if your choice is putting yourself and your children through divorce or living your life with someone who is repeatedly addicted, unfaithful, or abusive, choose divorce. You can heal from the wounds of divorce as will your children, but you choose to be continuously re-injured when you live with physical or emotional abuse. And, yes, repeated affairs or refusal to confront and deal with an addiction is a form of abuse.

So my advice to the thirty-something woman who sees her husband developing a problem with alcohol is to confront him and make it clear that you have no intention of living out your life with an addiction coming between the two of you. Don't wait fifteen years to deal with this problem. Start preparing yourself to be what you need to be in order to have the guts to leave if it becomes necessary. Work on yourself while you are asking him to quit, and waiting with hope. You are never wasting time if you are bettering yourself by getting strong either intellectually, physically, or spiritually. The woman who has an education, a solid faith, an established career, and good friends and family support is going to be less anxious and have more self-confidence if the marriage ends.

QUESTIONS AND SUGGESTIONS

Questions: If you were given truth serum, what would you say about the quality of your marriage? Can you identify what is and what is not working for you in the marriage?

Suggestion: Make a list of your partner's behaviors that work for you and the relationship, and then make another list of the behaviors that are not working for you. Are there any behaviors in the "not working for me" list that are "show stoppers," or behaviors that are dangerous to your spirit? If so, stop here and seek professional help. Otherwise, identify behaviors from this list that you honestly believe are personality traits and are not very likely to change. Put these under a heading entitled, "Need to Accept." One client's marriage greatly improved when she became intentional about accepting her husband's quietness and infrequent initiation of conversation, his dislike for parties, and his seeming lack of an adventurous spirit. Once she recognized these as "normal" behaviors for an introvert, she felt less resentful and irritated towards her husband; she accepted these as part of who he was (not about her) and learned new ways to get some of her social needs met through girlfriends.

Question: Did you have any behaviors left in the "not working for me" column? (Ones that didn't go in the "need to accept" list?)
Suggestion: For instance, if you had something like "doesn't help out around the house" left in this column, write it on a separate page. Now write down three headings under "doesn't help out around the house"— (1) Where (2) When (3) How. Under the heading "where" you will decide where you will assertively address this need for change with your partner. You'd probably want to address this at home while he is sitting in his favorite chair. I'll give you a hint for the "when" column. You don't want to bring it up when he walks in the door from work in a foul mood. Find a time when the kids aren't around, he has had time to unwind, and he isn't attending to his favorite activity. Now under "how" (how you will address this unwanted behavior) write out a clean assertive request stating what you think, how you feel, and what specifically you need from him. "I think it's unfair, I feel resentful, and I need for you to _____. If he agrees to your request, follow up by asking for a commitment. "Can I count on you for that?" You'll need to do this for all of the "need to change" behaviors. You'll get more of what you need if you ask. Hint: Don't ask for everything at once. Prioritize.

Question: What are your agreed-upon "couple" boundaries?
Suggestion: Sit down with your spouse and discuss the boundaries that you already have and any that you feel are needed in order to protect your partnership. For instance, have you spoken out loud your need for him not to have repeated lunches with another woman? Have you agreed to the need for regular dates (with no kids) for yourselves in order to keep your own romance alive? Have you said out loud what you consider disloyalty, unfaithfulness, or cheating? Have you talked about other things that you could do in order to "protect" your partnership?

10

The Affair—A Major Fairy Tale Buster

Nothing will kill the fantasy of the fairy tale any faster than the realization that your prince or princess is having an affair. The myth of the rescue, the false feeling of safety, and the promise of eternal happiness are destroyed when one partner discovers that the other partner has deceived him or her with this ultimate betrayal. Instead of a gradual realization that there is no "happy ever after," an affair can hit the unsuspecting woman very strongly, leaving the faithful partner reeling with disillusionment, disappointment, and fear.

Instead of a gradual "coming into their own" where they willingly and intentionally take back the responsibility for their own happiness, victims of affairs are forced to suddenly, without warning, face this harsh reality. The harmed partners have to face pain and heartache brought on by the very one that promised to love and honor them, the one that was the source of happiness. There is real loss when our hopes and dreams of how we thought things would be are snatched away from us. When the death of the fairy tale is sudden, the shock waves can resound for years to come. The loss is great and it has to be grieved. If you are suffering this hurt be gentle with yourself.

THE SEVEN HURTS OF THE AFFAIR EXPERIENCE

Suspicion

Since recent statistics show men are more often the straying partner, we will look at this experience's impact through women. It should be said, however, that there are growing statistics that women also choose to have extramarital affairs. Sometimes a woman will come into my office for counseling because she has become suspicious that her husband is having an affair. Usually by the time she is willing to see a therapist, the suspicions are pretty strong and well grounded.

Leslie, one woman who was facing the situation, came into my office complaining of anxiety, lack of adequate sleep, inability to concentrate, and a poor appetite. Within minutes she revealed that she was pretty sure that her husband was having an affair; she just wasn't sure. He was acting differently, using his cell phone in the basement, going to the gym more often, and she had noticed a charge on his credit card bill from a jewelry store…and Leslie hadn't been given any jewelry. One of her friends had seen him sitting in his car with a woman in the parking lot outside the hospital where he worked. But how could she be sure? I offered Leslie three choices: she could stick her head in the sand and go into denial, confront him and ask, or hire a private investigator.

The suspicion stage can go on for months or even years if a woman is locked up in fear – irrationally believing that she can't handle the truth. By failing to confront or investigate, she unwittingly enables the affair. If you suspect an affair, don't allow yourself to be endlessly tormented; do something. If you don't have adequate support from family or friends, seek help from a professional counselor.

Denial

Fear can drive a woman into denial even when the truth is staring her in the face. Fear can cause a perfectly intelligent woman to interpret seemingly obvious information in a completely contrary manner.

Darlene was such a woman. After giving me information that clearly indicated that her husband was probably having an affair, she rationalized that her husband was just overly warm and friendly with people. She rationalized that he never allowed her to go on business trips with him because he feared she might get bored. (His trips included places like Las Vegas, New York, and Los Angeles.)"He said I wouldn't have a good time and he doesn't want to worry about that." She rationalized a large volume of phone calls from his cell to his secretary's home phone. He said, "my business day doesn't stop at 5:00. I have to deal with things at the office twenty-four/seven."

Darlene did get up the nerve once to ask her husband if he was perhaps a little too close to his secretary. He responded by telling her that she was just insecure and paranoid; she convinced herself that he must be right. When she first arrived in my office she told me that she wanted counseling because she was too insecure. Yes, she was in fact insecure in that she did not have adequate trust in herself and her own knowledge. Instead of listening to her own inner voice, she listened to him. But she knew what she knew, and by the end of our session she had convinced me.

There are a number of factors that will determine whether a woman goes into denial or immediately deals with the information pointing to an affair. Obviously, women who are passive, fear confrontation, or lack assertiveness skills might lean toward denial. They erroneously believe that they can't handle the truth. These women may need more validation from friends, family, or a professional counselor. Women who are more emotionally and financially dependent are more vulnerable and more likely to deny the evidence that is staring them in the face. The wife who has never worked outside of the home, lacks training or education, lacks her own financial resources, or has poor self- esteem is likely to avoid the truth as long as possible. Her financial concerns may be quite valid, but her fears that she can't cope are often irrational.

Another factor in denial is the degree to which the couple has stayed connected or the length of time that the couple has lost their emotional tie. A woman who has not felt emotionally bonded to her husband for two years or more might be willing to risk confrontation. Some of my clients have said that they were relieved to discover that their husband was having an affair because now they felt justified in leaving. On the contrary, a woman might fear and dread facing the reality of an affair if she is still very much in love with her husband. It doesn't mean that she will automatically choose denial, but she will definitely have more difficulty facing the truth.

Confrontation

There is risk to confronting before investigating. If you confront and your partner denies, then you might be left with your suspicions…but now he knows you're aware and he may just be more careful. However, if your husband has no prior history of cheating, and has no history of lying to you, you might want to give him a chance to confess before going any further. It has been my experience that a few will confess without full proof, but most will deny it without hard evidence to the contrary. Leslie said that her husband had always been honest with her and she decided to confront him with her suspicions. She wasn't sure about how she would handle it if her husband denied an affair, but his explanations were not adequate to soothe her nagging suspicions. I assured her that she was an intelligent woman, and if she had seen the signs this time, she would see them again, and if signs of an affair continued, she could then hire a private investigator.

The next time I saw Leslie she had indeed confronted her husband and asked him directly if he was having an affair. He adamantly denied it and attempted to rationalize the changed behaviors that she had noticed. Leslie was not relieved by these denials and his explanations had not satisfied her. She had gotten braver. She searched for the truth and checked his cell phone bill, noticing multiple calls to a number that she soon discovered had been made to a woman. Her suspicions grew. Once she realized that her husband was not going to truthfully answer her suspicions, she hired a private investigator in hopes of getting the real story.

Investigation

It is my opinion that it is in a woman's or man's best interest to hire a professional investigator if their partners deny an affair in the face of significant evidence to the contrary. She should hire an investigator before confronting if her husband has a history of lying or cheating. She has the right to have the truth; without the truth she doesn't know what she's dealing with. Leslie hired a reputable investigator who suggested that she announce to her husband that she would be visiting her sister, who lives out of town, the next weekend. Her absence created an opportunity for him to be with another woman, if in fact there was one. From the investigation, Leslie got confirmation regarding her suspicions. She now had hard evidence of an affair and could approach her husband.

Although professional investigation is often the best route, I have seen some women become obsessed with their own surveillance and spying activities. It seems to become addictive for some and likely a distraction and avoidance from the real emotional pain. Obsession with spying becomes a way of avoiding the grief and the hard decisions that must be made. These women believe they never get quite enough evidence, and they get stuck in the anxiety-provoking stage of investigation.

Abigail was a beautiful young woman who was in denial about her husband's unfaithfulness. Telling me what had transpired had convinced me, yet she kept saying that she just wasn't sure. She was clearly miserable because her inner fears of losing him kept bugging her; she clearly didn't want to face the truth. In our weeks of counseling she gained strength and one day announced that she had taken her husband's computer to an investigator who had cloned his hard drive. Her suspicions were confirmed as emails and graphic photos revealed the truth to her in black and white and full color. She was surprised to find that she had the courage and the strength to cope with the truth that she had been avoiding.

Discovery and Realization

So now you know. After suspecting for weeks or months, you finally know. The realization both relieves you and scares you. Knowing is so different than suspecting. There is no standard reaction to discovering the truth of an affair. I've seen some clients go numb, some cry for days, some go into a rage, and some jump back into denial. "Well, he said she was just a special friend."

Regardless, the belief in the "happy ever after" is irreparably damaged. No matter what "he said," you know what you know. The bubble is burst and the pedestal is broken. It's very common for women to get hung up on wanting and needing to know details of the affair. It's as if, once they have faced the reality of the ultimate betrayal, they are now ready to see and hear it all, just how betrayed they really are.

Confronting with hard evidence is different than confronting with suspicion. However, don't be surprised if the lying continues. I've observed that many cheating spouses will only admit to the things that you have concrete evidence to support. This is further damaging to the relationship that has already taken a very big blow. If the lying continues after you have confronted your partner with evidence, my research and experience shows that you will not be able to repair the relationship and move toward reconciliation. Because…you know.

Crisis

When most couples experiencing affairs come into my office, they are in crisis. The affair has been confronted and either acknowledged or proven through investigation. The couple's balance is disturbed and all focus in on the affair. The betrayal has changed everything and shaken every belief that the woman had about her partner or her marriage. She doubts everything. She is wondering now if there have been other betrayals that she didn't know about and she doubts everything that comes out of his mouth. It is common in my practice to hear a woman go back years and put new meanings on things she saw in her husband in the past, things that she didn't attend to at the time. Like a computer, her brain keeps hitting the "back button" to try and make sense out of the mess she's in today.

For the younger woman who is not secure in her true self and purpose in life, it is common during this crisis phase for her to throw herself desperately at the betraying spouse. Her underlying fear that she can't survive without him might drive this behavior regardless of whether he is truly repentant and has accepted full responsibility for his deceptive behavior. When this happens there is often a false "honeymoon" stage where the real issues might be covered up or washed over, sort of like "make-up sex." Everything gets neatly swept under the rug, making it more likely that it will happen again.

I have often heard women say that they feel like fools after discovering evidence of a partner's affairs. I assure each woman that she is never a fool for expecting and trusting someone to be honest and forthright with her. She does, however, behave foolishly if she goes into denial and tells herself she can't handle the truth or that she can't go on without her partner. Truthfully, it will be very hard, but she can survive, whether he leaves or stays, or whether she decides to leave or stay.

Remember, you are never a fool for being victimized; it is what you do about it that is either foolish or wise. Sticking your head in the sand, failing to set clear boundaries, or allowing yourself to be victimized repeatedly is foolish. I want to remind you that his bad behavior is about him, whatever is going on with him right now, and the choices he is making about how to deal with it. Even if the marriage was riddled with problems, his bad choice to handle it by deception and betrayal is not about you.

The good news is that a crisis can be a window of opportunity. With the relationship being shaky and off balance, things are more flexible and pliable. There is the possibility for movement in a better direction. In the mist of great emotional pain and upheaval you might not be able to see the possibilities or you may be too emotional to trust your own judgment. If your marriage is in crisis, or if you suspect your spouse in involved in an affair and you feel unable to handle the difficult issues, seek professional help for the many decisions you will need to make.

Decision

The agonizing decision to leave or stay and work it out has to be made. As I mentioned earlier, some people react too quickly out of fear and try to continue their relationship as it was before the affair, making no fundamental change. There are numerous factors that must be weighed in the decision to leave or stay. The first and foremost requirement for considering staying in the relationship is whether the betraying partner is truly repentant and takes full responsibility for his or her actions.

Jeannie, a recent client of mine, wanted to keep her marriage together but her betraying spouse blamed her for his affair. When confronted with the affair, he presented her with a laundry list of things that he could not tolerate in her or her behavior. "He never really said he was sorry for the affair, but instead, pointed out all of my flaws and things that he says have bothered him for years." Jeannie got caught up in defending herself at first, taking the blame for their crisis. Later, however, she became angry as she recognized her husband's failure to assume full responsibility for his actions.

The second criteria for considering reconciliation is that all contact with the other person cease. This is tricky because you are immediately asking, "But how will I know?" You will have to risk trusting him if he is truly sorry and agrees to no further contact (as opposed to arguing against it). Clarify what you are asking him to commit to. "I'm asking you to have no contact, and that means no emails, no phone conversations, no text messages, and no meetings." Don't hesitate to ask him if he has talked to her again, if he's seen her again, or corresponded with her in any way. Yes, it is a risk, but with your eyes wide open and your head out of the sand, you will likely find out if he is lying. If he is saying he wants to stay in the relationship, inform him that this is the first test of trust and that you are counting on him to fulfill this commitment not to have further contact.

The third thing to consider is the question of repeated offenses. If your spouse has never cheated, is truly sorry, and owns his mistake, then there is hope that trust can be rebuilt. If he has had two prior affairs, you might want to consider the "three strikes and you're out" rule. Your chances of rebuilding trust go down proportionately with the number of affairs.

If you see a pattern of adultery, it's probably time to bail out. If you are mature enough to take responsibility for your own happiness, then why would you set yourself up to rely on someone who has a pattern of being unreliable? Why would you trust someone with a record of untrustworthy behavior? Why would you suddenly believe someone who has a pattern of lying? If you are unable to leave a relationship with a repeated offender who will not seek professional counseling, then you should seek professional counseling.

The fourth piece of your decision to leave or stay should concern your partner's willingness to reveal the truth of what happened. He can't continue to deceive or keep secrets and expect you, the victimized partner, to put yourself in a place of real vulnerability, working to trust while knowing you could be hurt again. Without full disclosure, the hurting spouse is left with nagging doubt and the belief that his secrets with the other woman are held as more valuable than her trust. The cheating husband may rationalize that his wife might leave if he confesses all, but he must be willing to take that risk if he is asking her to take a risk by trusting him again.

In my experience the wife will indeed react with hurt or anger at the initial revelation of new facts, but in the end feels a deeper level of trust and intimacy with her husband. She will value his willingness to take such a big risk for her. A client will often complain that her partner is defending the other woman, protecting her from hurt, while they are reeling with pain because of the disloyalty and deception.

A word to the wise: Keep the focus on the offense and the offending spouse; it doesn't do a bit of good to focus on the other woman. She wouldn't even be in the picture had your husband set appropriate boundaries. Focusing on her only serves to take the focus off of the real issues, the ones he can do something about.

Reconciliation/or Separation

The reestablishment of trust and growth toward real intimacy is possible after an affair when there is no more contact with the other person, there is full disclosure, no established pattern of cheating, and the offending spouse is truly sorry, taking full responsibility for his or her bad choice.

Once you have decided that there is hope, you must face the work and risks ahead of you. This is a prime opportunity to make counseling a requirement for your spouse who wants to reconcile. It is too easy to slip back into old patterns of behavior unless there is conscious and intentional work for change. Sometimes a man who has had an affair needs to be counseled individually in order to get support for the risks that he must take to regain his wife's trust or to help him if he is ambivalent himself. He must give up the affair, and must get off of the fence in order for real reconciliation to occur. Therapy can help support this as the only workable choice if the marriage is to be saved.

The road to reestablishing trust is long and hard and takes a commitment from both parties. In order to rebuild trust, the offending spouse must be willing to live his life as an open book. He must understand that secrets breed mistrust. A man who doesn't want you to ever look at his appointment book, come to his place of business, or be in the room when he is reading his email or answers the phone does not engender trust. A woman who has difficulty confronting should seek the help and validation of a therapist in order to establish new boundaries after her partner has had an affair. Poor boundaries may have enabled an affair and she may have been listening to what "he said" instead of what she knew. She may need a lot of validation for trusting her own knowledge of where boundaries are needed and trusting her own instincts to know and admit when they are broken. Trust can not be established if she is afraid to confront it when boundaries are crossed.

If during the decision phase you are even considering separation or divorce, seek immediate counsel from an attorney. Don't wait until you've made a major mistake before you seek legal advice. Pay for a consultation before retaining an attorney, and then, should you decide to reconcile, you haven't paid a lot of money for wasted advice. Since getting more information adds to your ability to make a good decision, it is better to have a legal consultation the minute separation is a consideration.

Should you decide that reconciliation is not possible, be self-caring as you go through this life-altering process and behave like the kind of person that you hope and dream to be. Get counseling for yourself if you need it, get good legal advice, seek out support from friends and family, and take care of yourself spiritually and physically. Many women who I see through this process finally see light at the end of the tunnel—light they felt they'd never see. They are always amazed at where they've been and how far they've come, but mostly, they are amazed at their own strength.

GRIEVING THE LOST DREAM

Darlene, a client who I saw through the trauma of her husband's affair, gained more and more knowledge and insight about her husband during the investigation. The more she learned, the more she started to view him as a scoundrel. At the end she said that she was glad to have found out who he really was and glad to be out of the relationship. She also asked, "Then why do I feel so bad?" I talked to Darlene about her feelings and told her she was grieving—not the loss of this dishonest man, but the loss of her hopes and dreams of how she thought things would be. She thought she would be married forever. Maybe she even thought she would be cherished and happy forever. The realization had set in that these were false dreams and life as she knew it was over. When a dream is lost, it must be grieved.

THE AFFAIR AND THE STAGES OF GRIEF

I have observed in my counseling that Elizabeth Kubler-Ross's stages of grief apply to people whose partners have had affairs. First, there is the shock and denial. "This can't be happening to me." We've discussed in the previous section (and like all of the stages of grief) it is only a problem if you get stuck there. Grief, and therefore all of its stages, are normal, but it becomes dysfunctional when the grieving person gets stuck and fails to progress to the next stage. Unlike the stages of an affair that I have outlined previously, the stages of grief apply after the affair has been confronted and the decision to leave or stay has been made.

Many women are surprised by the fact that they are experiencing grief after they have seemingly weathered the worst. They faced their suspicions, confronted, made their decision and came through the crisis. But they ask themselves: *Why am I sitting in a therapist's office now that I've made it through the affair and its aftermath? Why am I struggling with these feelings of sadness, anger or guilt?*

Denial

One of my clients, Shannon, sat in her chair next to me in my office looking rather dazed. She did manage to keep her wonderful sense of humor, however. She began to talk of her trying experiences with her partner. "My life has been like one of those "B" rated movies or one of those crazy soap operas; I can't believe this has happened to me. I can't believe this is my life." She had in fact dealt with her husband's affair and made her decision to work toward rebuilding their relationship. Shannon was now beginning to deal with her grief. The "happy ever after" dream was lost forever. It wasn't as if she could never be happy again, but she knew that it would never be the idealistic kind she has previously envisioned.

It's important to remember that even if giving up the fairy tale makes us better, more responsible and capable of navigating our own life course, we don't give it up without some grief. The first stage of grief says: *"I can't believe this is happening to me."*

Anger

Shannon had not completely dealt with her anger earlier in handling her husband's affair. She was caught off guard. Things moved so quickly when her husband confessed and immediately showed true remorse that she buried her angry feelings within. She was so afraid of losing her husband and breaking up their family that she wouldn't let her anger show; it might push him back to the other woman. She began working hard to repair their broken relationship without processing her anger. Now she felt safe to let it out. In the anger stage we're saying: *"How dare you do this to me."*

Anger is a natural part of grief, but if it is suppressed it will only delay progress. I warn my clients against suppressing anger, as it will only resurface when you least suspect it. In my office Shannon had a safe place to begin to process her anger about the betrayal, the hurt, and the loss of her dream for a "happy ever after." If the hurt partner buries angry feelings, the angry feelings sometimes get displaced onto someone else, like "the other woman." When this happens, the resurfaced anger is redirected and processed.

There are people who came out of denial, get angry and stay angry for the next twenty years. If you see yourself getting stuck in any stage of grief, seek professional help to free yourself to move on towards acceptance of the life event that you can't go back and change. Be aware that what you can change is yourself and the way that you allow the past trauma and hurt to continue to interfere with your one and only life. Decide not to become bitter in spite of great wrong that was done to you. Make a conscious intentional decision to heal yourself; take full responsibility for your own happiness.

Bargaining

The bargaining stage can be closely related to the denial stage: *"Maybe it wasn't as bad as it all appeared. Maybe she just pursued him relentlessly; it wasn't his fault."* You are trying to juggle things in such a way as to find them more acceptable. A woman might also get caught up in thinking that she can change something about herself that will prevent his infidelity in the future. "Maybe if I just get a boob job, he won't ever cheat again. Maybe if I just show him more affection, he won't look elsewhere." In this stage the victim of an affair can erroneously take the responsibility for her husband's behavior and place it on herself, thinking that she can fix it or prevent it from ever happening again. Yes, she may need to participate in repairing the damaged relationship by changing many of her own behaviors that contributed to a sick marriage, but he alone must assume responsibility for his poor choices in handling his own unhappiness through deceit. She can't fix him or take responsibility for his choices.

Depression

Shannon worked through her anger. At this point she had gotten over the shock and dealt with her anger only to find herself feeling significantly depressed. "I can't figure out why I'm so depressed now that we seem to be doing better and getting back into a better stage of our marriage." I told her that her feelings were quite normal. When we can no longer deny our loss and we come face to face with just how angry we really are, we can become depressed. As we acknowledge that life will never be the same, we doubt at times that we can bear it. What we are saying at this stage: *"The hurt was too much; how on earth will I ever trust again?"*

If depression is about hopelessness, why would a betrayed partner feel depressed when things seem to be looking up? We feel hopeless about things we cannot change; we may heal from an affair, but we will never be able to change the fact that it happened. We face the permanence of an unchangeable event—there it sits in the road—even after you've passed it by, it's still just sitting there. Some women seem to focus their doubts of ever trusting again on themselves. We'll discuss more about an affair's affect on self-confidence later in this chapter.

Acceptance

The final stage of grief is acceptance. The betrayed partner now has insight and gained acceptance. This stage says: *"It happened and I can deal with it."* Whether you are working to repair the relationship or waiting for your soon-to-be "ex" to sign the final divorce papers, in this stage you believe that you will survive. Once you come to acceptance you are ready to move on with life, together or separate. It doesn't mean that you will never revisit any of the other stages, but it means that most of the time you will be making progress. You haven't forgotten about what happened, but you are now thinking about it 10 percent of the time instead of 80 percent of the time. If you see a movie about straying partners you may have a touch of old hurt that you felt before. But now, instead of overwhelming you with intense pain, it is just a pang. You find that it is happening less often.

I often hear the question from my clients, "How long am I going to feel this way?" I can't tell the suffering partners how long they will feel the ache, but I can tell them it won't be forever. For a woman in a marriage that she believed was going well, and who loved her husband and trusted him, she will experience a bigger shock than the woman who was in an unsatisfying marriage with someone she didn't trust. For a woman who perceived her husband to be honest (he never cheated before), it will probably be more devastating than for the woman whose husband has cheated before. Usually, the greater the shock, the greater the hurt, anger, and depression, and the longer the road to acceptance. The grief experience is not universal, however, and no hard fast rules or predictions can be made. A grieving person may not go through the previous stages in a nice straight line. We often jump back into a previously experienced stage, perhaps finding ourselves angry again after getting through the stage of depression. Grief isn't so neat and ordered. In spite of being quite messy, grief is normal and necessary for healing, accepting and getting on with our lives.

The Affair and Damage to Self

My Looks

Brandi's husband has been having an affair with a younger woman. Brandi and her husband are in their early forties; his girlfriend is twenty-six. The hardest part of the whole thing for Brandi has been the effect it has had on her self-image. "I doubt everything about myself now. I feel perhaps I should have breast implants. I feel I'm not pretty enough, thin enough, and my hips are too big." Brandi saw her husband's interest in a younger woman as clear proof that her own looks were inadequate. She tuned out any evidence that didn't fit this distorted view that was solely based on her husband's poor choice to have a fling with a younger woman. Therapy helped her get back to a realistic view of her self and come to a rational belief that her husband's choice to have an affair with a younger woman wasn't about any flaw in her, but was about his own flaws and issues. Although Brandi was realistic about her own behavior that affected the marriage, she could now realize that her husband's choice to have an affair was about him, who he is, and how he deals with the world. In time, Brandi started recognizing feedback from other sources that validated her original view of herself as quite adequate.

My Personality

Faced with a marital betrayal, some women doubt their appearances while others may doubt aspects of their personalities or actions. Heather's husband had an affair, and when confronted, lambasted her with criticism about her behavior over the sixteen years that they were married. Instead of dealing with her feelings about the affair, she questioned herself and everything she had ever done or said to her spouse. She began to doubt her adequacy as a mother, a wife, a person. It distracted her from the more pressing issues. In order to see the situation clearly we need to conclude that we are not talking about whether or not Heather did in fact have faults that her husband found unacceptable. In reality, he may have had some legitimate complaints. However, his unhappiness with her actions could not be solved by lying and cheating with another woman.

The affair has to be dealt with before partners are able to approach each other about needed changes. Otherwise, requests for a partner's change in behavior come across as blame or justification for the affair. Ideally, Heather's husband would not have built up sixteen years of resentment about some of her behavior, but he would have asserted his need for change at the time something offended him. He would now have to learn to protest differently so that he would not repeat the same pattern of built-up resentment and passive-aggressive coping–an affair.

Jayne's partner had been experiencing this destructive behavior pattern. Jayne came to see me for counseling several months after her husband had admitted to an affair. "We saw a counselor in Charlotte, but he just wanted to work on our communication skills, and I wasn't able to deal with my anger and hurt about the affair." Don't be afraid to assert your need to process the affair should you find your counselor moving too quickly to address shortcomings in the way you and your partner relate. A good counselor will want you to have adequate time and support for dealing with your hurt, anger, and trust issues. If the relationship is to be repaired, both the current crisis as well as the preexisting marital issues must be addressed.

Friends

Friends are a great resource if self-doubt hits you after a partner's affair. Girlfriends will remind you of who you really are and help you once again see your good points. They will validate good thinking and tell you when you're getting a little crazy. "But I'm afraid to tell anybody." In my counseling practice I see both – the women who share and seek support from friends, and the women who keep it all to themselves. My professional experience reveals that the ones who tell a trusted friend, a sister, or a pastor do better. Dealing with a major life crisis with virtually no support will leave you void of needed feedback and validation. If the person who has lied and cheated is the only one that you have to listen to, you will struggle much harder to regain your confidence.

I often have women clients tell me that their husbands forbade them to tell anyone. It may be in his best interest to keep the affair a secret, but it is not likely in your best interest since you need and deserve the comfort and validation of a trusted person who is concerned with your well being. Seek validation from friends and family if you feel your confidence slipping or your view of self confused or damaged. If self-doubt becomes a serious problem, seek professional help.

The Trust Factor

The biggest hurdle after an affair is the trust issue. It can plague the hurt partner for years after the affair. The less confident a woman was before the affair, the more difficulty she will have with trust. She may not trust herself to know if her husband is lying or cheating again. Trusting yourself is a prerequisite to trusting your spouse. You must trust your gut instincts and your own good sense to recognize red flags or to simply access resources. Research indicates that the more intelligent you are, the more likely you are to access counseling or other resources in a crisis. You don't have to trust yourself to be psychic, but you have to trust yourself to figure out where to go when you don't have the answers.

If you have shared with friends or family you will have resources for checking out your fears, suspicions, or concerns. Although we do need to express our doubts aloud to our spouse, it is helpful to have other outlets since expressing every little doubt might be counterproductive. Counseling can be helpful in balancing between the need to ask about and rehash details of the affair with reinvesting in the marriage by allowing positive experiences and feelings to happen.

The Wound

If you think of the damage caused by an affair as an open wound, you can think more clearly about how to treat it. The wound has to be examined thoroughly and cleaned out. It hurts to clean a wound. It stings.

If all of the dirt is out, then it is less likely to get infected and do more damage. If we place a bandage over a thorn or chunk of dirt, it will fester. The cleaned wound then has to be dressed; the crisis and pain of cleaning and examination is over. In time, a small thin scab of new skin forms over the wound. However, every time we start picking to look for more dirt, the wound is reopened— more pain and more time for healing. Good counseling after an affair offers a safe place to examine the wound and get the dirt out, in order for healing to begin. But that's just the beginning. After this crisis work is done, the marriage must be examined and old wounds may need to be revisited.

Often the couple is very defensive after being damaged by an affair, defending themselves against further hurt. This can make it hard for them to be vulnerable enough to show their tender feelings or to expose their flaws that might be hurting their spouse. If the affair is addressed successfully in the crisis stage and the wound receives sufficient ointment, the couple can open up sufficiently for real healing to begin.

Open Book Policy

Problems with trust will diminish in intensity over time if the offender is living his life as an open book. This means that there is not secretiveness, but openness…easily done when there's nothing to hide. After an affair, it will aid the healing process if the offending partner does not show anger when questioned by his spouse. Remarks such as,"Why are you an hour late from work?" should be said without anger and defensiveness. Defensive responses will only increase mistrust, not reassure. Patience on the part of the partner who has been deceitful will help rebuild trust. This is of course assuming that the criteria for reconciliation talked about earlier have been met and that the offender has ended all contact with the other party, told the truth, accepted full responsibility for his actions and has a humble repentant attitude.

Damage to Our Daughters

Girls, particularly teenage girls, are also greatly damaged by a parent's affair. Abby, an eighteen-year-old college freshman, told me that she has trust issues with guys since her father cheated on her mother and left her for another woman. She doesn't ever feel relaxed in a relationship and fears she will be fooled or deceived. Teens are often lacking in confidence anyway, and this kind of damage further erodes their trust in themselves. "If my mother was fooled, then I can be fooled." The daughter feels as deceived as the spouse because she trusted her father to be looking out for her best interest and she doesn't see the divorce, the break-up of her family, as being in her best interest. Now *all* guys are suspect.

Long before an affair takes place, the man has often disconnected from his spouse and sometimes his family as well. It is sometimes this disconnection, this lack of involvement in their lives that is more damaging to girls than the affair itself. Think about it. What does a father do to validate his son's masculinity? He plays sports with him, roughhouses with him, or participates in other masculine activities with him. How does he validate his daughter's femininity? He tells her she's pretty; he makes her feel prized, like she's worth spending time with. The disconnected father isn't making his daughter feel important or worthy. "I didn't feel that close to my dad before, but it's worse since the affair." Her first important relationship with a male has left her feeling "less than."

When this relationship comes up drastically short, the young woman may even doubt that anything better exists. Do not neglect to offer counseling to your teen if the family is in crisis due to an affair. Tell her that you would like for her to commit to three sessions, and after that she can decide for herself if she wants to continue.

Children need not know about an affair unless you are definitely separating, meaning somebody is moving out. Even then, the details of the affair are not to be shared with children. Seek support from friends, family, or a professional counselor, not your children. If the marriage might be repaired (the offending spouse is sorry and you want to try to mend the marriage), then the children don't need to know at all. Why put them through the distress of marital difficulties that they can't relate to or can't fix? Don't make the mistake of making a child your sounding board.

When your fairy tale fails because your partner has an affair you can feel like you've been in a bad accident, dazed, hurt, angry that it happened, and depressed in hopelessness about your future. Professional therapy will help. Be willing to invest the time and money in yourself and your future by seeing a counselor.

QUESTIONS AND SUGGESTIONS

Question: Have you been in denial about numerous pieces of evidence pointing to the probability that your spouse is having an affair?
Suggestion: Talk to a friend, family member, or counselor about your suspicions in an effort to get them validated. It will become clearer whether your suspicions are valid or if you are reading way too much into something. If others find the behaviors equally suspicious, then you will want to proceed to confronting, or, if there is a history of dishonesty, hire a professional investigator. Action is required in order to get out of denial. Talk to somebody.

Question: Have you confronted your spouse with your suspicions about his affair only to have him tell you that you are paranoid?
Suggestion: Everybody with suspicious thoughts is not paranoid. You're only paranoid if you think suspiciously in the face of no evidence that something's wrong. Men often lie to women and then tell them they are insecure when they are questioned. Women clients often tell me that they sensed something was wrong, even before the pieces of evidence presented themselves. If he denies, and your gut, based on red flags and

pieces of evidence, tells you that he's having an affair, go straight to your local private investigator. You can check an investigator out with the Better Business Bureau.

Question: Is your spouse telling you to trust him in the aftermath of an affair but hiding his cell phone bill, appointment book, or calling you paranoid when you ask why he's late?

Suggestion: This calls for real assertiveness. Tell your spouse how it feels when he has been deceitful (the affair and all of the lies involved) and then calls you names when you ask questions that could offer reassurance. Tell him that you need for him to live his life as an open book if he is asking you to trust him after a major breech in trust. Before asking him about something that concerns you, tell him that you are struggling with doubt and asking for reassurance. Then tell him what you need to know in order to be reassured. If his harmful behavior continues after you have become more assertive in asking for what you need, make couples counseling a requirement in order for you to stay in the marriage. You cannot trust a partner who is secretive, particularly after the disloyalty of an affair.

Conclusions

What I Wanted

Betty Friedan, a major figure of the woman's movement, died last year. Through my research and in my practice with women, my own passions for women's empowerment have been stirred, and I now have a new appreciation for the stand she took. Friedan's book, *The Feminine Mystique*, has impacted all of us, whether we realize it or not. Agree or disagree with it all, or in part, women reap the benefits of her work done on our behalf. I no longer take for granted the rights that have been won for women through the persistent toil of people such as Betty Friedan. You don't have to be the same race, religion, or espouse the exact same philosophy to know that her passion and purpose made a positive difference. I want other women to know that: We don't all have to act alike, look alike, or think alike in order to all want equal respect and to all make an impact on changing our little corners of the world.

Two of the quotes by Friedan which have had great meaning for me are:

"Age is not 'lost youth' but a new stage of opportunity and strength."
"It is easier to live through someone else than to become complete yourself."
(Source: *ThinkExist. com Quotations*. "Betty Friedan quotes.")

I knew this message (of not having to act or think alike) was coming across loud and clear when my two sons started calling me a conservative Christian feminist. For too long, feminism has been a bad word among conservatives and Christian women. I am both, and I clearly and proudly call myself a feminist. I support a doctrine advocating social, political, and economic rights for women equal to those of men – a dictionary definition of feminism. Frankly, I believe that one of the tales still told to women is that it's not "Christian" to be a feminist. If Christ were walking the earth today, I believe that he would abhor the malicious control, manipulation, and behaviors that show a lack of true respect for women by some men. A "giving up and giving in" response to this lack of real respect keeps many women from being all that they could be. I want women to see that when they succumb to this, or give in to this behavior, they are closing themselves off from the discovery of their own true selves and the realization of their own power.

There are numerous explanations offered in this book as to why women devalue themselves and perpetuate a societal status of "less than." Most importantly, I want you to keep in mind that things don't always continue for the same reason they start. You can now get credit at the bank without a man's signature. You can apply for any job you want, whether your husband approves or not. The original constraints are gone, but the old attitudes and beliefs are dying slowly. Very slowly.

I hope you will get a sense from reading this book of personal responsibility for your part in enabling and perpetuating the old attitudes toward women. Decide you will either comply with "less than" treatment or you won't. We must all accept the challenge to change ourselves and not wait for the world to change for our convenience. The challenge is to behave as if you are not "less than" and refuse to accept "less than" treatment by others.

Part of healing our society is to heal our relationships with one another. But we must first heal ourselves. Our self. I can't love others until I learn to accept and love my self; to make my self whole. Put Humpty Dumpty back together again. To make my self whole, I take back the parts of me that I have given away in hopes of making others happy with me. Find your own dreams, passions, and purpose. Be in possession of all the pieces in order for there to be wholeness.

I am currently in a small women's group that focuses on spiritual growth. We are presently utilizing a book entitled *The Cup of Our Life* by Joyce Rupp. At first I thought the "cup" analogy was a little hokey. However, it's turned out to be quite meaningful for me. When I see my life as a cup—sometimes empty, chipped, misshapen, or dirty—I can also see that same cup getting a good scrubbing or a missing piece glued back, or getting filled. The whole congruent self and the seeking, searching soul will find a God-given passion and purpose for living.

Where I'm Going…

I rejoice that I can comfortably and boldly say…I have no idea. I say it with faith and comfort because my intent – to be useful and act with purpose—is clear. Not knowing where I am going no longer causes me anxiety because I now realize that I don't need to know the outcome in order to get started; I just have to be willing to act on what I know now. The outcome will evolve with my increase in knowledge, the people I encounter, and my experiences along the way. I will try to keep myself open to new and different thinking. I know that other sparks will be ignited. New dreams will be turned into goals.

It is my hope that this book will prompt you to undertake a journey of self-discovery and make an intentional movement toward gaining a congruent self. Where am *I* going? In search of a life filled with faith, passion, and purpose. I hope you will all come with me!

EAST ORANGE PUBLIC LIBRARY
3 2665 0036 1381 9